BHAKTI MARGA

SECOND EDITION
Printed in Germany
ISBN 978-3-940381-43-9

www.**bhaktimarga**.org

Sri Swami Vishwananda

SRI GURU GITA

Commentary on the great mysteries of
the Guru-disciple relationship

ॐ प्रेमअवताराय विद्महे
सत्गुरुदेवाय धीमहि
तन्नो विश्वानन्दा प्रचोदयात्

om premavataraya vidmahe
sat gurudevaya dheemahi
tanno vishwananda prachodayāt

We meditate on the Premavatar,
we fix our minds on the Satguru.
May Sri Swami Vishwananda inspire us.

Jagadguru Sri Mahavatar Babaji

Satguru Sri Swami Vishwananda

The *Sri Guru Gita* is a part of the *Skanda Purana* written by Veda Vyasa. The *Skanda Purana* is one of the 18 Puranas, and comprises the praises that show us how to open up the heart to receive Grace. There are 400 verses in the *Guru Gita* but we will discuss only the most important ones, which number 182.

The *Sri Guru Gita* is a discussion between Lord Shankar and Parvati, wherein Goddess Parvati asks Shiva, "Who do you consider the greatest one on Earth?" Lord Shiva, in the form of Dakshinamurti, explains to Maha Devi that the greatest form on Earth is the form of the Master.

Krishna Himself said in the *Bhagavad Gita*, "I am the embodiment of the Guru. It is through My Grace that the Guru appears on Earth. And it is through My Grace that the disciples are guided to where they belong." Christ also said, "I have come for my sheep. I have come for my flock." So, wherever one is, the Guru will search and will attract the disciple.

The *Sri Guru Gita* is one of the most wonderful songs, because all that we are doing here to please the Divine Mother [*Swamiji is referring to the Navaratri Celebrations of 2014*], is happening through the Grace of the Master.

Athā Śrī Guru Gītā prarāmbhaḥ

Now the Guru Gita begins.

OM asya śrī gurugītā
stotra mantrasya
Bhagavān sadāśiva ṛṣiḥ

OM. Lord Shiva is the Rishi, sage and seer of the mantras in this hymn known as the Guru Gita.

Nānāvidhāni chandāṁsi
śri guruparamātma devatā

The rhythms of this hymn are diverse. Its deity is the Guru, the Supreme Self;

Haṁ bījam saḥ śaktiḥ kroṁ kīlakam
Śri guru prasāda siddhayarthe
jape viniyogaḥ

'Ham' is its bij mantra, 'Sah' its Shakti. 'Krom' is its mystery, its magic. Chant this hymn repeatedly to attain the Guru's Grace.

Athā dhyānaṁ

Now we meditate.

Haṁsābhyāṁ parivṛtta patra
kamalair divyair jagat kāraṇair
Viśvot kīrṇamaneka dehanilayaiḥ
svacchandam ātmecchayā

Taddyotaṁ padaśāmbhavaṁ tu caraṇaṁ
dīpāṅkura grāhiṇaṁ
Pratyakṣākṣara vigrahaṁ gurupadaṁ
dhyāyed vibhuṃ śāśvatam

The Guru's Lotus Eyes are represented by 'Ham' and 'Sah'. He is the Divine Origin of the universe. Of His own will, He manifests in numerous forms to uplift the world. He is ever-free. His form is imperishable, everlasting and all-pervading. Meditate on His Lotus Feet.

Mama catur vidha puruṣārtha
siddhyarthe jape viniyogaḥ.

I chant the Guru Gita for the realisation of the four goals of life: Dharma (righteousness), Artha (wealth), Kama (desire) and Moksha (salvation).

Sūta uvāca:

Verse 1

**Kailāsa śikare ramye
bhakti sandhāna nāyakam
Praṇamya pārvatī bhaktyā
śaṅkaraṁ paryapṛcchata**

*Suta said:
Once, while Lord Shiva, who knows the secret of devotion, was seated on the beautiful Mount Kailash, Parvati bowed to Him with reverence and asked:*

"Lord Shiva, who knows the secret of devotion." Here we have to note that the secret of devotion is known through the sadhana. And Lord Shiva is considered to be the greatest of all *sadhaks*, because He is in constant meditation. He is always meditating on Narayana, because everything comes from Narayana. So Lord Shiva, because of His devotion, because He is submerged into His *sadhana* - that's why in this verse He is referred to as the one "who knows the secret of devotion".

Because devotion is not just superficial, there is deepness into it. Even if it appears very plain - sometimes you have devotion, but you don't feel much; you are praying and you say, "My prayer is mechanical." But in reality it is not! Because even the uttering, the chanting of the Divine Names is not merely superficial, it has its depth. Its depth is cleansing the impurities which one has carried throughout many lives.

So, here Bhagavan Shankar is saying that He is the one who knows that deepness, that secret of devotion, because He is fully submerged into bhakti. He is fully absorbed into that devotion, which means that He is enjoying bhakti! Because if people are not absorbed into their devotion, then they get bored of it. But if you know the secret which lies behind what you are doing, you will love to do it! That's why when you love to do something, it bears different fruits. Behind everything that you do, there is a certain secret! And by knowing that secret, you will enjoy whatever you do.

Here Bhagavan Shankar is enjoying His devotion to Lord Narayana, because He knows the secret behind that. That's why we can say that He is the embodiment of sadhana Himself.

Suta continues describing the scene, as Lord Shiva "was seated on the beautiful Mount Kailash, Parvati bowed to Him with reverence and asked" - here you have to see that Mount Kailash stands for the topmost spiritual level. It's not just a place, a mountain, but it stands for a high level of spirituality.

Bhagavan Shankar is seated there together with Parvati. Here you see the two qualities, Shiva-Shakti, the form and the formless. Shiva is considered to be the formless and Shakti the manifest; so both go hand in hand, Purusha and Shakti. Parvati, who is the manifestation of Shakti, asked Lord Shiva, with deep reverence and humility, to explain the deepness which lies within the one whom Lord Shiva is meditating on and which aspect it is.

Śri devy uvāca:

Verse 2

OM namo devadeveśa
parātpara jagadguro
Sadāśiva mahādeva
gurudīkṣāṁ pradehi me

The Goddess said;
O Lord of Gods! O Supreme preceptor of the universe!
O benign and benevolent Mahadev, God par excellence!
Unravel and explain to me the mystery of the Guru.

Here the Goddess said, "O Lord of Gods! O Supreme preceptor of the universe! O benign and benevolent Mahadev." Here Goddess Parvati, as Shakti, is asking the Purusha. She is addressing Lord Shiva as the Lord of Gods - you see, Narayana is eternally the Supreme Lord, the Supreme God Himself. Then, He manifested Himself three-fold as Brahma, Vishnu and Shiva; Brahma deals with creation, Mahavishnu with preservation and Shiva with dissolution. Among these three, Mahavishnu is the direct manifestation of Narayana. That's why He sustains everything. Brahma is also a manifestation, Shiva is also a manifestation, but they are His co-workers.

There is not much happening with Brahma, because He is just creating. The greatest work is to sustain the creation! It is easy to create something, but to sustain, to make that thing work is more difficult, no? That's the work of Mahavishnu. And then of course Lord Shiva is the dissolution. He removes everything so that a new reality may come into being. Therefore, destruction is not just to destroy and finish! Destruction means also a renewal of things. That's why Devi refers to Him as the Supreme preceptor of the Universe, because through destroying, He is also allowing creation to happen.

The Goddess carried on saying, "God par excellence! Unravel and explain to me the mystery of the Guru." Here the Goddess is asking, "You are the Lord! You praise the Guru! You who are the greatest – the Deva of devas, the demigods all praise you! You who are the dearest to Narayana, the dearest to Mahavishnu! Please explain to me: what is the secret that a Guru holds? Why is a Guru different from anybody else?" So even the Goddess Herself needs to know and understand that.

Verse 3

**Kena mārgena bho svāmin
dehi brahmamayo bhavet
Tvam kṛpāṁ kuru me svāmin
namāmi caraṇau tava**

*The Goddess said;
O Lord! My salutations at your Lotus Feet. Tell me by which path a human being can become one with the Absolute? O benevolent great God!*

Here the Goddess carried on asking, "O Lord! My salutations at your Lotus Feet. Tell me by which path a human being can become" - can attain the Lord, the Supreme Narayana? O merciful One! O Deva, Lord of the demigods! Explain to me the secret of the Master and by which path a human being will be saved.

Bhagavati knows that the mind of man is constantly creating karma. Each breath is creating karma. Each action, each thought is creating karma, so the Mother is very concerned. She is concerned for everybody! That's why She is asking the Absolute how can one attain the Lotus Feet of the Lord? How can one attain the Grace of the Lord?

Seeing such a devotion in Her and Her concern as a Mother for Her children, He said:

Īśvara uvāca:

Verse 4

Mamrūpāsi devi tvaṁ
tvat prītyarthaṁ vadāmyaham
Lokopakārakaḥ praśno
na kenāpi kṛtaḥ purā

Īśvara said:
O Goddess, You are My very form and self! I answer and explain this out of My Love for You. No one has ever before asked Me this question for the benefit of all the lokas (worlds)..

Bhagavan Shankar said, "O Goddess, You are My very form and self!" Here Lord Shankar - Shiva is explaining to Parvati that there is no difference between Him and Her. Even if they are separated into two forms yet they are One! She is the very form of Himself. Not only in the form, but even in the Self Itself - Shiva and Shakti are One. That's the same as when we say that Radha and Krishna are One.

Lord Shiva said that He will explain this mystery. He will explain what lies behind this secret of devotion, the secret of the Guru. Not because She has asked Him, but because of the Love that She has for Him. So out of His Love for Her, He will explain the secret of devotion to Parvati.

Then He said to Her, "No one has ever before asked Me this question." She was the first one to ask Him this question. And by Him answering this question, it will be of benefit to all the universes, to all the lokas. The Sanskrit is *Lokopakārakaḥ*, which signifies that what Shiva will explain to Parvati is not just for Her ears. It is not only for Her to understand that. But, by Her understanding, all the lokas, all the universes themselves, will benefit from the blessing of it.

Verse 5

Durlabhaṁ triṣu lokeṣu
tacchṛṇuṣva vadāmyaham
Guruṁ vinā brahma nānyat
satyaṁ satyaṃ varānane

I reveal to You the mystery inscrutable of all the three worlds. O Beautiful One! Listen! The Absolute is not different from the Guru. This is the Truth. This is the Truth.

Lord Shiva said to Parvati, "I reveal to You the mystery inscrutable of all the three worlds." The greatest and deepest secret of all the three worlds. "O Beautiful One! Listen!" Here Bhagavan Shankar is addressing Goddess Parvati as the Beautiful One! He is saying that She, the creation, the Mother is the most Beautiful One. It is not only the outside beauty, but it is also the inner beauty. So, beauty here also means the most concerning, the most caring, the most joyful.

Bhagavan Shankar carried on, *Guruṁ vinā brahma nānyat*, which means, "the Guru is not different from the Absolute". So, the first thing that Lord Shiva said to Parvati was that there is no difference between the Guru and the Absolute. That's what Krishna said in the Gita, "I am in the form of the Guru." If people perceive a difference, then they are completely wrong. But if they see the Guru in that supreme state; if they perceive the Lord seated in the heart of the Guru; if they perceive that there is no difference between the Guru and Him - they will attain Bhagavan Himself.

So, here Bhagavan Shankar is saying, "The Absolute is not different from the Guru. This is the Truth." And this is the reality! *Satyaṁ satyaṃ varānane*! If one sees the difference between the Guru and the deity, then one is in delusion. But if one perceives the Guru as the deity, then one is in the Truth.

Verse 6

**Veda śāstra purāṇāni
itihāsādikāni ca
Mantra yantrādi vidyāśca
smṛti ruccāṭanādikam**

This is the Truth not revealed by the Vedas, various other scriptures, epics, the sciences of mantra and yantra, magic formulas, etc., or the smritis and other sources.

Here Bhagavan Shankar carries on explaining that this Truth is not revealed by the *Vedas*, or by various other scriptures, epics, the sciences: it's not revealed by mantra; it's not revealed by yantra. It's not even revealed by tantra or by any other sources. Bhagavan Shankar Himself is saying that the *Vedas* don't tell you about this Truth. It will tell you about it partially, but the revelation of it only happens when one surrenders to the Feet of the Master. That's the only way to get the revelation. Because without surrendering to the Lotus Feet of the Master, then it's just words which one reads or words which one talks about. Then it doesn't make any sense.

Verse 7

**Śaiva śāktāgamādīni
anyāni vividhāni ca
Apabhraṁśa karāṇīha
jīvānāṁ bhrāta cetasām**

The Saivite and Shakta treatises and different sects and dogmas only further confound the already deluded creatures.

Here Shiva said that there are many paths: the Saivites, the Shaktas, the Vaishnavas, the Ganapatyas, the Kaumaras, the Brahmanas and more. There are different groups, different schools, different ways, different theses, different sects, different dogmas, which very often say different things on the outside; but in the deepness, when one surrenders, when one attains the Lotus Feet of the Master - one crosses over the delusion of the dogmas; one crosses over the delusion of the outside; for the reality reveals the Absolute Inner Self.

So here Bhagavan Shankar is explaining that there are different paths, different ways of thinking, but all these ways come from the Guru.

Verse 8

**Yajño vrataṁ tapo dānaṁ
japastīrthṁ tathaiva ca
Guru tattvamavijñāya
mūdhāste carate janāḥ**

Those who perform sacrificial rituals, take vows, do penance, offer gifts, perform japa and go on pilgrimages without knowing the Truth of the Guru are ignorant.

Here Bhagavan Shankar carries on explaining, "Those who perform sacrificial rituals, take vows, do penance, offer gifts, perform japa and go on pilgrimages" - He is saying that all these are very important! It's important to perform sacrificial rituals. It is very important to take certain vows in life, to do penance, to offer *dakshina*, to offer gifts, to do your *sadhana*. *Mūdhāste carate janāḥ* here means that all of these are very good, but they become useless if you don't know the Truth of the Guru. So if one goes through all this without knowing the Truth of the Guru, in this verse Lord Shiva says that they are ignorant.

Verse 9

Gurur buddhyātmano nānyat
satyaṁ satyaṁ na saṁśayaḥ
Tallābhārthaṁ prayatnastu
kartavyo hi manīṣibhiḥ

The Guru is not different from the Self, from Consciousness. This is beyond doubt the Truth, the Absolute Truth. Hence a wise man must feel it his duty to seek and find the Guru.

Here Bhagavan Shankar carried on explaining the Truth saying that you should know the deeper Truth of the Guru before you go on pilgrimages, before you do your sadhana. You should know that the Guru is not different from your True Self, from the Consciousness. There is no difference. Because the Guru is the Absolute Self Itself inside the bhakta.

Satyaṁ satyaṁ na saṁśayaḥ; this is beyond doubt the Truth, the Absolute Truth. He is saying that you don't need to see the Guru outside only, but you have to recognise that the Guru is the Self inside of you.

Tallābhārthaṁ prayatnastu kartavyo hi manīṣibhiḥ. Here He said If you are wise you should know that your soul's duty is to seek and find the Guru.

Verse 10

**Gūḍha vidyā jaganmāyā
dehe cājñānasambhavā
Udayo yatprakāśena
guruśabdena kathyate**

Owing to ignorance, the embodied being thinks that the Universal Mother resides in the body as secret knowledge. But She reveals Herself in Her own Light, with the Grace and through the words of the Guru.

Bhagavan Shankar is saying that owing to ignorance those who don't have knowledge, the people, the embodied beings, think "that the Universal Mother resides in the body as secret knowledge." Bhagavan Shankar is saying that if you are looking inside of you plainly without surrendering to the Master, thinking that everything is inside of yourself and you don't need anybody then you are completely in ignorance! You are completely in delusion! You are completely in untruth!

Udayo yatprakāśena guruśabdena kathyate; because of your search for the reality, for knowledge, "She reveals Herself in Her own Light." But She reveals that Light through "the Grace and through the words of the Guru." This means that because of your willingness to search you go on pilgrimages, you do japa, you do your sadhana - automatically She brings you to the Feet of the Master.

Verse 11

Sarva pāpa viśuddhātmā
śrī guroḥ pādasevanāt
Dehī brahma bhavedyasmāt
tvatkṛpātharṁ vadāmi te

Through service at the Feet of the Guru the embodied soul becomes purified and all its sins are washed away. It becomes one with the Supreme. I disclose this to you out of Grace.

"Through service at the feet of the Guru the embodied soul becomes purified and all its sins are washed away." So here Bhagavan Shankar is saying that the easiest way to wash the sins and to purify yourself is to surrender to the Feet of the Master. This is the easiest way. You see that in the life of many saints.

During the *Gita* course we talked about Dukhi Krishna. He didn't have any mantra, nothing! He didn't ask anything from his Guru, but he had just surrendered himself to his Guru. At the age of fourteen he surrendered to his Guru's Feet and listened carefully to what the Master asked of him. The Master didn't give him big, big sadhana to do, but in the most simple way, he just told him to water the plants. By simply taking the word of the Master and watering the plants he received the Grace of Srimati Radharani.

So here Bhagavan Shankar says, *śrīguroḥ pādasevanāt*, which means that only through service at the Feet of the Guru one's sins are cleansed and one is purified. One attains the Supreme Lord because one becomes like Shiva. One attains this state of Shivoham. So you become also the great bhakta where the Lord reveals Himself inside of you.

But here Bhagavan Shankar is saying that this happens only through the service at the Feet of the Master! It will not just happen coincidentally. It will not just happen because God said, "Okay, today I decided to bring you on the spiritual path, just like that." No. It happens because of your willingness to surrender. Because service to the Feet of the Master is not out of fear or out of imposition. No. It has to be out of Love! Because the relationship between the disciple and the Master is a relationship of this Love. So it's due to that willingness of serving the Master that the Grace and purification happens.

Tvatkṛpāthaṁ vadāmi te, here Bhagavan Shankar says to Parvati that He is revealing this reality to Her out of Grace, out of Kripa. Because here He is not talking to Her, as Shakti. He is talking to Her as creation. He is talking to Her as each individual person. That's why He used the word 'Grace', "I disclose this to you out of Grace." Grace is very important. Bhagavan Shankar is emphasising that without Grace whatever one does will not lead anywhere. But through Grace, She will carry you. Grace is like the Mother who carries the child.

Verse 12

Gurupādāmbujaṁ smṛtvā
jalaṁ śirasi dhārayet
Sarva tīrthāvagāhasya
samprāpnoti phalaṁ naraḥ

If a man sprinkles the water at the Guru's Feet on this head, remembering the Lotus Feet of his Guru, he obtains the punya, merit, of bathing in all holy waters.

Here Bhagavan Shankar says, "If a man sprinkles the water at the Guru's Feet on this head, remembering the Lotus Feet of his Guru, he obtains the *punya*, merit, of bathing in all holy waters." By taking the Charanamrita - the water which has washed the Feet of the Master - and by sprinkling it over oneself, it's like taking a bath in the Ganges.

In the Hindu tradition we believe that by taking a dip in the Ganges we are purified from many lives of sin, many lives of stains, many karmas are being purified. You see, Ganga took its source from the Lotus Feet of Narayana

Himself. Then, from the Lotus Feet of Narayana, She entered the kamandalu of Brahma. She was sent to Earth when Sage Bhagirath performed his penance. Why did Sage Bhagirath perform the penance? It was to free his ancestors; not himself, but his ancestors. Here Bhagavan Shankar is saying that by taking the water which has washed the Feet of the Master and by throwing it over oneself, this is equivalent to taking a bath in the Ganges. This also means that it doesn't only purify yourself, but it's purifying previous generations as well. It has the same effect.

Verse 13

Śoṣaṇaṁ pāpa paṅkasya
dīpanaṁ jñāna tejasām
Gurupādodakaṁ samyak
saṁsārārṇava tārakam

The holy water (that has washed the Guru's Feet) dries the slush of sins, lights the lamp of knowledge and helps one cross the ocean of earthly life.

The Charanamrita, the holy water which has washed the Feet of the Master dries the power of sin; it removes the power to sin from the bhakta and it lights the Light of knowledge. This is the power of the Charanamrita: it gives Divine knowledge, the knowledge of the True Self and liberates oneself. It makes one cross over the ocean of delusion and reach the life purpose, the goal of your incarnation.

Verse 14

Ajñāna mūla haraṇaṁ
janma karma nivāraṇam
Jñāna vairāgya siddhyarthaṁ
gurupādodakaṁ pibet

It uproots ignorance, which is the consequence of avidya, 'not knowingness', puts an end to rebirth and (its cause) karmas. One should sip the holy water of the Guru's Feet for Enlightenment, resignation and unattachment, vairaagya.

The Charanamrita uproots ignorance in the bhakta; ignorance, which is the cause, the root, the consequence of avidya (foolishness, ignorance). When this ignorance is removed, it makes way for liberation. But if one stays in that ignorance, one is always in the cycle of birth and death. One always stays in this cycle to be reborn again and again, many lives. But if one has the knowledge, one ends the karma and this cycle of rebirth.

So here Bhagavan Shankar is saying, "One should sip the holy water of the Guru's Feet for Enlightenment, resignation and unattachment, *vairāgya*." Here sipping the water doesn't literally mean to drink the water, but to take *aadesh*, the instruction from the Master. The instruction, which the Master gives, one should take it, sip it! One should meditate on it! One should absorb oneself into what the Master says.

Verse 15

Guroḥ pādodakaṁ pītvā
gurorucchiṣṭa bhojanam
Gurumūrteḥ sadā dhynaṁ
gurumantraṁ sadā japet

Drink the holy water of the Guru's Feet; eat the leftovers of the food offered first to the Guru. Constantly meditate on Him and constantly repeat the mantra given by the Guru.

Here He says, "Drink the holy water of the Guru's Feet; eat the leftovers of the food offered first to the Guru." *Gurorucchiṣṭa bhojanam* - the Prasad of the Guru should be eaten, because the Prasad which the Guru has eaten has the infusion of His blessing into it.

"Constantly meditate on Him and constantly repeat the

mantra given by the Guru." *Gurumūrteḥ sadā dhynaṁ* - He says that your dhyaan should be continuously on the form of the Master.

Gurumantraṁ sadā japet - the japa that you have to do is what the Guru has given you, not just plainly chanting hundreds of mantras. When you receive the mantra from the Guru, chant this mantra only - that will be the cause of your purification, that will be the cause of your liberation.

Verse 16

Kāsī kṣetraṁ tannivāso
jāhnavī caraṇodakam
Gurur viśveāśvaraḥ sākṣāt
tārakaṁ brahma niścitam

The very place where the Guru resides is Kashi. The holy water of His very Feet is the Ganges. The Guru is the Lord of the universe, Shiva Himself. He is indeed the Saviour, Brahma.

Kāsī kṣetraṁ tannivāso means that where the Guru dwells is Kashi itself. Where the Guru is - is Vrindavan. Where the Guru is - is the holy Tirtha itself. All the holy pilgrimage places are where the Master lives.

Jāhnavī caraṇodakam, here Bhagavan Shankar is saying that the holy water of His very Feet is the Ganges itself.

Gurur viśveāśvaraḥ sākṣāt tārakaṁ brahma niścitam; the Guru is the Lord of the universe, the Trimurti Itself is personified in the form of the Master. He is indeed the Saviour, Brahma. The Guru is the personification of Brahma, Vishnu and Shiva. And He is manifested to save humanity. He has incarnated to bring all to the supreme state, to bring all to the Lotus Feet of the Lord.

Verse 17

Guroḥ pādodakaṁ yattu
gayā'sau so'kṣayo vaṭaḥ
Tīrtha rājaḥ prayāgaṣca
gurumūrtyai namo namaḥ

The holy water of the Guru's Feet is Gaya, the Akshaya (imperishable) banyan tree, the most sacred Prayag. Salutations again and again to the Guru!

Guroḥ pādodakaṁ yattu gayā'sau so'kṣayo vaṭaḥ, here He said that the holy water of the Guru's Feet is Gaya. It is also an imperishable banyan tree.

Tīrtha rājaḥ prayāgaṣca gurumūrtyai namo namaḥ, the

most sacred Prayag, which is the confluence of the three rivers, Ganga, Yamuna and Saraswati - where they meet is called Prayag. He said, "Salutations again and again to the Guru!" Bhagavan Shankar Himself is praising the Guru saying that the Feet of the Master is Prayag itself. If one is surrendered to the Master's Feet there is no need even to go to Prayag.

If one has surrendered to the Master's Feet, the Master becomes the wish-fulfilling tree, the kalpataru and Gaya is where Narayana's Padam is present. In the Hindu tradition people go to Gaya to perform the last rites for death; it is said that when you do the last rites for death there, you get liberated. So here Bhagavan Shankar is saying that the Guru's Feet is Gaya itself. If you are surrendered to the Guru's Feet, Gaya is there. So liberation is at the Feet of the Master.

Verse 18

Guroḥ mūrtim smarennityaṁ
gurunāma sadā japet
Gurorājñāṁ prakurvīta
guroranyanna bhāvayet

Meditate ceaselessly on the form of the Guru. Always repeat His name, carry out His orders and think not of anything except the Guru.

Guroḥ mūrtim smarennityaṁ gurunāma sadā japet, here Bhagavan is saying again that one should constantly, ceaselessly, with deep devotion and love, continuously meditate on the form of the Master. Not only meditate, He also said to chant continuously, repeat, do japa with the name of the Master.

Gurorājñāṁ prakurvīta guroranyanna bhāvayet means to carry out His orders. Carry out what He says without questioning; carry out what He asks with love and humility. Don't think of anything else than the Master.

Verse 19

Guruvaktra sthitaṁ brahma
prāpyate tatprasādataḥ
Guror dhyānaṁ sadā kuryāt
kulastrī svapateryathā

The Supreme Knowledge abiding on the Guru's lips can be realised through His Grace alone. Always meditate on the Guru, as a loyal wife unremittingly thinks of her husband.

Guruvaktra sthitaṁ brahma means that Brahma Himself resides in the lips of the Master. And whenever the Guru graces one with these lips, one gets realised.

Guror dhyānaṁ sadā kuryāt kulastrī svapateryathā; "The Supreme Knowledge abiding on the Guru's lips can be realised through His Grace alone." Here Bhagavan Shankar is saying that what the Master says has a lot of meaning, it has a lot of understanding. Because as you know very well, we can interpret Sanskrit in 24 different ways. How would you know how to interpret it? Very difficult! If there are 24 ways of looking at it, it will be very difficult. He said that you can understand what the Guru says only by the Grace of the Master Himself. This means that to receive that Grace is very important. But to receive that Grace one has to be surrendered.

Bhagavan Shankar carried on saying, "Always meditate

on the Guru, as a loyal wife unremittingly thinks of her husband." *[Audience and Swamiji burst out laughing and audience claps enthusiastically]* So, how many wives constantly think of their husbands? In ancient times the wives performed Sati, you know? They were always surrendered to the feet of their husbands. Nowadays the wives think: where is the husband? What is he doing? With whom is he? *[Audience laughing]* It is not meditating, it is doubting! *[Swamiji and audience laugh]* But here He is reminding that when you love someone, what is in your mind? That person is constantly in your mind, no? Wherever you go, whatever you do, that person is dear to you, is very important to you! The person is very close to your heart. That's what it means. Let's look at it in ancient times' way, when people were very dedicated. But even now, it is like that when you are freshly in love. I say 'freshly' because it is like this at the beginning, then in the 'middle' it changes and afterwards... forget it! But when you are 'freshly' in love, you are constantly thinking of the one you love, the one you are with. There is not a moment that you are not looking at your phone waiting for the SMS, Telegram or WhatsApp. And when you get it you are happy, because it is dear to you! Here Bhagavan Shankar is saying that one should meditate constantly on the Guru's form. There is nothing else that one should put the mind on other than the Master.

Verse 20

Svāśramaṁ ca svajātim ca
svakīrti puṣṭi vardhanam
Etatsarvaṁ parityajya
guror anyanna bhāvayet

Set aside your station and stage in life, caste, fame, wealth or means of attaining worldly success. Think of nothing but the Guru.

Bhagavan Shankar is saying that when you are meditating on the Feet of the Master, on the form of the Master, you should put everything else away. Whatever stage of life you are, in whatever caste you belong, whatever you want to achieve in life, fame, wealth, name, worldly success - when you are concentrating on the Master, when you are meditating on the Master, your mind should not divert. Your thought should not wander around. *Guror anyanna bhāvayet* means that your thoughts should only be focused on the Master, on the Guru. There should be no other thought than the Guru. So when you are meditating on the Guru's form, all outside things should stay outside and you should see the Master inside of your heart.

Verse 21

Ananyāś cintayanto māṁ
sulabhaṁ paramaṁ padam
Tasmāt sarva prayatnena
guror ārādhanaṁ kuru

The supreme state is easily attainable for him who meditates on his Guru with single-minded devotion. Strive utmost to adore and propitiate the Guru by all means.

The supreme state, the highest state is easily attainable for the one who meditates with single-minded devotion on the Guru, with deep focus, with the mind not wandering around. With the mind fixed at the Feet of the Master, with devotion, everything becomes easy. *Tasmāt sarva prayatnena guror ārādhanaṁ kuru*, for that to happen you have to try your best to adore and propitiate the Guru. So, here you see that it is not just to say plainly, "Oh, I accept this Guru as my Guru, and that's it!" Here Lord Shankar Himself is saying that one must by all means, by all effort - even if the mind is wandering around, the mind should be brought always to the form of the Master. And once you do that, everything becomes easy; but this doesn't happen just in one go. It takes effort from your side. Because without the effort from your side it becomes in vain. Who will give you something knowing that you will not be able to handle it? Nobody! But if somebody knows that you can handle something, then they will give it to you. For example, you have a business, you go to the bank and ask for credit. But the manager looks at you and thinks, "This man will never give me back my money! He will never pay back the credit." Do you think he will give you the credit? He will never give you the credit. But if you have certain qualities, certain characteristics, then just by looking at you, the manager will say, "Yes! This one is ready!" Then he will give you the credit. The same with the Guru: as long as one is not ready, one must try by all means to be ready to receive the Grace.

Verse 22

Trailokye sphuṭa vaktāro
devādyasura pannagāḥ
Guruvaktra sthitā vidyā
gurubhaktyā tu labhyate

Gods, demons, or cobras of all the three worlds spell out clearly that the knowledge abiding in the Guru can be acquired only by total devotion to Him.

The gods, demons, all the lower species of the three worlds, all who have the True Knowledge of the greatness of the Master, they all spell out clearly the greatness of surrendering to the Lotus Feet of the Master with devotion to Him. They all know that only through total devotion and dedication one attains the Lotus Feet of the Master. Not just randomly, because nothing happens just by coincidence. As Bhagavan Krishna said in the *Gita*, "All happens by His Will." He places each one where they have to be. He places each soul according to the category of one's karma and according to the category of one's devotion; He places one in that particular womb and He traces the way that will lead to liberation.

Trailokye sphuṭa vaktāro devādyasura pannagāḥ - He says that all the species, the demigods, the asuras, the demons and the lower species all know that without surrendering to the Master it is impossible to free themselves. That's why you will see that in the Hindu tradition even the asuras have their Guru to guide them. Even with their pride they know that there is a hierarchy. The demon Shukracharya is the Guru for the daityas and He also gives good advice to them. When the pride of Lord Shiva manifested itself in the form of Jalandhar, Shukracharya told the demons, "Don't go and fight Him because He is Lord Shiva Himself!" But what did they do? And as He was a very dear associate of Jalandhar, He told him, "Jalandhar, you are also a part of Lord Shiva, why are you going to fight with Lord Shiva? You can't! Because you are a very low quality of Him, you are a lower manifestation of Him, you'll never win." So Shukracharya was warning him, "You'll be killed. Don't be a fool!" So you see, even He was giving them good advice - not to go and fight someone greater, that they could not handle. Even the demons know about the greatness of the Master. If you have this knowledge, only then will you be given True Knowledge.

Verse 23

Gukārastvandhakāraśca
rukāras teja ucyate
Ajñāna grāsakaṁ brahma
gurur eva na saṁayaḥ

The first syllable 'Gu' means darkness and the second, 'Ru', Light. The Guru is doubtlessly Brahma who dispels all darkness.

The first syllable 'Gu' means darkness and the second, 'Ru', means Light. So Parabrahma, the Ultimate, residing in the heart of the Master is the dispeller of darkness. Here you see that the word 'Guru' holds both: darkness and Light. So the Master has mastery over both. The Master has mastered darkness, transcending it, to bring Light to the bhakta. If the Master had not transcended darkness, how would He have power over it? So this means that the Guru has mastered both; He is the Master of the darkness and the Master of the Light. And at the same time, *Ajñāna grāsakaṁ brahma gurur eva na saṁayaḥ*, which means that He is above that. He has mastered the darkness, He has mastered the Light, yet He is residing above the darkness and above the Light. So that's how the Guru dispels the darkness of ignorance in the one who surrenders to Him. Because if a Guru can't bring someone to the state of God Consciousness, then that is not a Guru. That's a teacher and not a Master!

The Hindi word 'guru' means teacher. But, you have different levels of teachers. You have the *shishya* guru, which means the guru who teaches a particular subject. For example, if you want to learn English you go to an English teacher; if you want to learn French you go to a French teacher. But the shishya guru can't teach you how to get rid of your pride and your ego. So, even if the direct translation of the word 'guru' is teacher, there is a big difference between a shishya guru and a Satguru.

Verse 24

Gukāraḥ prathamo varṇo
māyādi guṇa bhāsakaḥ
Rukāro dvitīyo brahma
māyā bhrānti vināśanam

The first syllable 'Gu' is suggestive of the attributes such as Maya. The second, 'Ru', is suggestive of the Supreme Absolute who is free from the illusion of Maya. ('Gu' represents the lower manifested world while 'Ru', the Supreme Absolute, the Unmanifest.)

The first syllable 'Gu' has the attribute of Maya. 'Gu' also means ignorance. Here in this verse Bhagavan Shankar is saying that this first syllable 'Gu' stands for Maya Prakriti, Devi, the Shakti that binds and holds one to this reality. And the second syllable 'Ru' stands for Purusha, stands for the Supreme Absolute which frees one from illusion. So, in the same word you have both. In the word 'Guru' you have Maya and you have the One who frees you from Maya. So having both aspects inside, this shows that the Guru is the Master of Maya, Master of this reality. He knows how to free one from that reality and He knows also how to put one in that reality - both. Because to master it, you have to know both ways. You can't master something by knowing only one way; then you have not mastered it!

If everything goes beautifully - you live in a very fancy,

fancy reality, or in a dream reality, you will not know what true happiness is. Only when you master the other side, when you master the lower quality, then you will truly know the higher qualities.

Here Bhagavan Shankar is explaining that in the word 'Guru' there are both aspects: the Guru is the Master of Maya and at the same time He is Maya. So, He knows when to cast a shadow over somebody and He knows when to remove that shadow.

Verse 25

Evaṁ gurupadaṁ śreṣṭhaṁ
devānāmapi durlabham
Hāhā hūhū gaṇaiścaiva
gandharvaiśca prapūjyate

The Lotus Feet of the Guru are the highest object to be pursued. They are difficult even for gods to find and attain. The groups called Haha and Huhu and gandharvas worship them devotedly.

The Lotus Feet of the Guru are the highest object that one should strive for. Here Bhagavan Shankar is saying, "Don't strive for liberation." He is not asking you to strive for perfection. He said that firstly what you have to attain is devotion. You have to pursue devotion to the Feet of the Master. That should be the highest object. And here He is saying that to attain this highest object - to make this the highest object, it is even very difficult for the gods and the *asuras*. Even if they are completely surrendered to the Supreme Reality, they find it difficult to surrender to the Master's Feet.

Then He says, *Hāhā hūhū gaṇaiścaiva*, which means that the simple tribal people, through simplicity, through the humility of the heart, they find it very easy to worship with devotion.

For the gods and for the asuras it is difficult because they are so much into the mind, they are so much into their own things that it is very difficult for them to attain that devotion. Nevertheless, it does happen through the Grace.

However, through humility of the heart, for the human beings who surrender to the Feet of the Master, it becomes very easy due to that devotion that they have.

Verse 26

Dhruvaṁ teṣāṁ ca sarveṣāṁ
nāsti tattvaṁ guroḥ param
Āsanaṁ śayanaṁ vastraṁ
bhūṣaṇaṁ vāhanādikam

All these have the faith that there is nothing higher than the Guru. The aspirant should offer those seats, beds, clothes, ornaments, mounts and vehicles to the Guru, which would please him.

Dhruvaṁ teṣāṁ ca sarveṣāṁ nāsti tattvaṁ guroḥ param; all these, the ones who are humble in the heart, the simple ones, they have faith that there is nothing higher than the Guru. The simple people don't know God but they know the Master! For them God is far away. God is another higher level. They don't know about Him. For them God is the Master who is revealing God to them! And in the easiest way, the Master makes God accessible for them. The Master gives God to the people.

Āsanaṁ śayanaṁ vastraṁ bhūṣaṇaṁ vāhanādikam; these aspirants, they long so much for the Grace of the Master that they offer the seat, they offer beds, clothes, ornaments, mounts, land, vehicles, everything, to please the Master. Because there is nothing else that they want to reach, but the Ultimate. Even if they want to reach God, they know that without the Grace of the Master it is not possible. But, they know that with the Grace of the Master everything will be possible! That's why in this verse He said that they offer to the Master whatever they have, whatever they feel inside of their heart.

Verse 27

Sādhakena pradātavyaṁ
guru santoṣa kārakam
Guror ārādhanaṁ kāryaṁ
svajīvitvaṁ nivedayet

The Guru should be pleased and should be made happy. One should dedicate one's entire life to the Guru's service.

Sādhakena pradātavyaṁ guru santoṣa kārakam; "The Guru should be pleased and should be made happy." Here He said that the aim of a devotee, the aim of a disciple is to make the Guru happy and to please him.

Guror ārādhanaṁ kāryaṁ svajīvitvaṁ nivedayet means that when one has met one's Guru one should dedicate one's entire life to the service of the Guru. *Guror ārādhanaṁ kāryaṁ* means that only through the service to the Master, like in the story of Dukhi Krishna, which I told earlier (commentary of verse 11) - he didn't ask the Guru for any Guru Mantra; the only thing he asked the Guru was Guru *aadesh*, the order of the Guru. He was 14 years old and said, "Gurudev, order me!" And the Guru said, "Your duty is to water the plants only, nothing else." And he did it. For twelve years he did it! Without asking anything from the Master. And until the Guru talked to him again, there was a space of 12 years. Without even talking to the Master for 12 years, yet he was doing his duty with full devotion. After twelve years the Master himself, Sri Hridaya Chaitanya Das, called him and looked at him. Dukhi Krishna had hurt his head and there were worms coming out of his head. His Master said to him, "I am very pleased with your devotion!" Imagine how surrendered is that state! People are always thinking, "I, I, I, I, I, I". Here Dukhi Krishna forgot about everything, forgot about himself completely. What was inside of him was only the Guru, nothing else. He was completely surrendered to the service of the Master.

Verse 28

Karmaṇā manasā vācā nityam ārādhayed gurum Dīrgha daṇḍaṁ namaskṛtya nirlajjo gurusannidhau

Constantly serve the Guru with the mind, speech and action. Prostrate unabashedly like a stick in front of Him without the least reserve.

"Constantly serve the Guru with the mind, speech and action." Here Bhagavan Shankar is reminding that the duty of a bhakta, the duty of a devotee is to constantly serve, not only serving in the outside, but the mind has to be always into the state of service. He also said that the speech, what one has to talk, should always rotate around the Master. And the action has to be also in the service to the Master.

Dīrgha daṇḍaṁ namaskṛtya nirlajjo gurusannidhau, means that you should prostrate yourself without any shyness, lie down flat like a dry stick in front of the Master without any hesitation or reserve. Without any feeling of, "What my neighbour is thinking of me?" He said, "Prostrate flat wholeheartedly with the mind fully surrendered to the Master."

Verse 29

**Śarīram indriyaṁ prāṇāṁ
sadgurubhyo nivedayet
Ātmadārādikaṁ sarvaṁ
sadgurubhyo nivedayet**

Dedicate everything to the true Guru; the body, the senses, the prana. Offer everything you hold dear. Shed all sense of 'my-ness', mamakāra, and seek refuge in the Guru.

Here He says, "Dedicate everything to the Guru; the body, the senses, the prana," the mind, the intellect. Offer everything you hold dear to you. Don't keep anything! Offer the dearest things that you think that belong to you, which you feel that are the most important to you, offer it to the Master's Feet. In that way, you also get rid of the pride. Because pride, 'my-ness','I-ness', this which you say that belongs to you.

Ātmadārādikaṁ sarvaṁ sadgurubhyo nivedayet; He said we should offer this 'my-ness', this 'I-ness', this pride, this *ahamkara*, offer it to the Master. Offer this big 'I' to the Master and seek refuge at the Feet of the Master.

Verse 30

**Kṛmi kīṭa bhasma viṣṭhā
durgandhi mala mūtrakam
Śleṣma raktaṁ tvacā māṁsaṁ
vañcayenna varānane**

O Beautiful One! Do not hesitate to offer to the Guru all the body, which is full of germs, worms, waste matter, foul-smelling urine and faeces, phlegm, blood, and flesh, without sparing anything.

Here Bhagavan Shankar is addressing Parvati, "O Beautiful One! Do not hesitate to offer to the Guru all the body."

Offer yourself fully to the Master. Because what is the body? The body is "full of germs, worms, waste matter, foul-smelling urine and faeces, phlegm, blood, and flesh, without sparing anything."

So the body is made up of all this. And when you die the body decays. Are you this body or are you the Atma? Here Bhagavan Shankar is telling us to offer this body which we call ours, ours, ours - offer it, however it is, offer it at the Feet of the Master. Only by offering this body at the Feet of the Master, fully, one will be free!

Verse 31

**Saṁsāravṛkṣamārūḍhāḥ
patanto narakārṇave
Yena caivoddhṛtāḥ sarve
tasmai śrī gurave namaḥ**

Salutations to the revered Guru who uplifts souls perched on the tree of the world from sinking into the ocean of hell.

Salutations to the Guru who can free people from drowning themselves into delusion. Because if one falls into delusion, one for sure will attain hell, as delusion is equal to hell. Instead of being elevated you will be *hell-evated*. So the Guru elevates you but pride hell-evates you, takes you down.

Yena caivoddhṛtāḥ sarve tasmai śrī gurave namaḥ, meaning the Guru is the only one who can save you from drowning yourself into the ocean of delusion.

Verse 32

Gururbrahmā gururviṣṇur
gururdevo maheśvaraḥ
Gurureva parabrahma
tasmai śrī gurave namaḥ

The Guru is Brahma, He is Vishnu, He is Shiva. The Guru is indeed Parabrahma, the Supreme Absolute. Salutations to Him.

The Guru is Brahma, the creator. The Guru is Vishnu, the preserver and the Guru is Shiva Himself, the destroyer. The Guru is indeed the Supreme Parabrahma, Krishna Tattva, *Aham Gurubhyo Namaha*. That's how Bhagavan Krishna referred to the Guru saying, "I am the Supreme Brahman and I am the Guru Himself. I am the Absolute to the one who surrenders to Me in the form of the Guru."

So, salutations to Him; *tasmai śrī gurave namah*, praises be to the Feet of the Master.

Verse 33

Hetave jagatāmeva
saṁsārārṇava setave
Prabhave sarva vidyānāṁ
śambhave gurave namaḥ

Salutations to the Guru who is Shiva, the one ever auspicious and welfare-causing, the first cause of the universe, the bridge to cross the ocean of worldliness and the source of all knowledge.

"Salutations to the Guru who is Shiva, the one ever auspicious and welfare-causing." So salutations to the Guru who is always caring for the welfare of this world, who is always caring for the devotee.

Prabhave sarva vidyānāṁ śambhave gurave namaḥ; "the first cause of the universe, the bridge to cross the ocean of worldliness and the source of all knowledge." Here He says that the Guru is the bridge from this reality, from this material world to the spiritual world. Without the Guru there is a big gap; the Guru bridges the two worlds, the physical world and the spiritual world. Salutations to Thee, the one who bridges these two worlds.

Verse 34

Ajñāna timirāndhasya
jñānāñjana śalākayā
Cakṣur unmīlitaṁ yena
tasmai śrīgurave namaḥ

Salutations to the Guru, who with the collyrium stick of knowledge treats the eyes of one blinded by the darkness of ignorance.

When people are in darkness, they are in ignorance, they are like a blind man, who is walking around trying to find his way. But for the one who has a Guru, the Guru becomes like the stick for the blind man. The Guru becomes the light, the torch in the darkness lighting the way to salvation, lighting the way to reach God Consciousness.

Verse 35

Tvaṁ pitā tvaṁ ca me mātā
tvaṁ bandhustvaṁ ca devatā
Saṁsāra pratibodhārthaṁ
tasmai śrī gurave namaḥ

Thou art my father, thou art my mother, thou art my relation, thou art my God. Salutations to thee, O Guru, the imparter of 'Jyaana', True Knowledge, in this world.

Thou art my father, mother, relation and God. So this is the Guru. Once you find the Guru, the Guru becomes your mother, your father, your relationship, your God.

When you go to India, especially when you are on a spiritual path, someone may ask you what is the name of your father. Of course you will think, "My father is Robert," or "John". But in reality, when they ask you these questions - Who is your father? Who is your mother? – If you answer the name of your biological parents, then they know automatically that you are not on the right way. *[Audience laughs]* Because if you go to an ashram and they ask you, "Who is your mother and father?" then you should say the Guru's name.

If you are on a spiritual path, you are following your Guru, you know the name of your Guru, whenever someone asks you, especially if a Guru of a certain ashram asks you, "Who is your mother and father? What is the name of your mother and father?" You should never mention the father and mother of your material body, but you should always mention the Guru. But this happens only when you are fully surrendered, only then they will ask you these questions. And by asking you these questions they will immediately know how much you are surrendered to your spiritual path. How much you are surrendered to the Guru! Because, if you mention the names of your biological father and mother, then they will speak with you, but on another level. However, if they ask you, "Who is your mother and father?" and you answer, "My mother and father are my Guru *so and so*." then they will automatically say, "Okay, you belong on that path." You have a certain identity, you have a certain sense of belonging. Then they will realise that you are on the right way.

So in this verse He said, *Tvaṁ pitā tvaṁ ca me mātā*, which means that when you have found your Guru, there is no material father, there is no your material mother; but the Guru becomes the mother, the father, and the Guru Himself becomes God.

And this is also in the Christian tradition. When you go into a monastery, you have to leave your former life behind, completely! This means that the moment you take shelter at the Feet of the Master, you should let go of your former life. It doesn't mean that you have to finish everything. No. But inside of you - this is not outside, but it is inwardly - your life transforms; your life changes at that moment; it's a new birth.

That's what Bhagavan Krishna said in the *Gita*, when He referred to the 'twice born'. The 'twice born' doesn't refer only to the Brahmins. The 'twice born' refers also to the moment you take shelter at the Feet of the Master.

Christ also said, "To attain the Kingdom of Heaven, you have to be born again." This means that only by surrendering, only when you surrender to the Feet of the Master, like the apostles and the disciples of Christ surrendered (that's why He called them) - at that moment, a new life starts. Christ became the mother, the father and everything for them. If you look at the disciples, their mind was only and always rotating around the Master. Their talk was only and always rotating about the Master, nothing else! That's what St. Paul himself said, "I am born every day with Christ. I go throughout the day with Christ and I die with Christ. I resurrect every day with Christ." And this happens because they are disciples; they are not just devotees, but they are fully surrendered.

Here He also said, *Saṁsāra pratibodhārthaṁ tasmai śrī gurave namaḥ*, meaning all these qualities are achieved through "the imparter of True Knowledge". The Guru imparts to the disciple the True Knowledge of how to attain God and through that True Knowledge one is freed from the illusion of this world.

Verse 36

Yatsatyena jagatsatyaṁ yatprakāśena bhāti tat Yadānandena nandanti tasmai śrī gurave namaḥ

Salutations to the Guru whose existence is the cause of the world and its existence, whose Light (Knowledge) makes all creation perceptible, whose bliss makes all individual bliss possible.

Here Bhagavan Shankar is offering salutations to the Guru as it is because of the Guru that this world is still standing! Because the Masters, who have come throughout the centuries, since time immemorial, have kept the Sanatana Dharma, have kept Dharma alive, have kept this True Knowledge.

If Masters would have not incarnated, this world would be in perdition since a long time ago. So, that's why Masters have incarnated in the world, not only in India, but in different parts of this world, to remind people about the true purpose of life. And since time immemorial, from the beginning of existence itself They have kept alive the light of knowledge, the light of bhakti, the light of surrender. And through this light creation has carried on. Because without this Light, the world would have already ended a long time ago. It is only through the Grace of the Master that the world is still a better place. It is only through the Master's Grace that it is possible for each individual person to feel bliss.

Verse 37

Yasya sthityā satyamidaṁ
yadbhāti bhānurūpataḥ
Priyaṁ putradi yat prītyā
tasmai śrī gurave namaḥ

Salutations to the Guru, the cause of all creation, by whose form as the Sun and Light all becomes perceptible and in whose Love all relationships (like father-son) become dear.

Here He says that it is through the Grace of the Masters, through the Grace of the Guru, that one perceives the Light of Love, True Love. Not just plain love, but the deepness of Love. So, through this Light of the Master, all relationships become dear. Because it is not just a relationship of the outside, a blood relationship. Here He says that in the Guru's family everybody becomes dear, which means that the Guru unites you all, from wherever you all are. This also means that all of you have been coming together for many lives.

You may come from Russia, from France, from Italy,

from Spain, from America, Latin America, Brazil... North Pole, South Pole *[Swamiji says this in a joking way and audience laughs]* So it is only through the Grace of the Master that people come together. He is bringing everybody into one family. The Guru becomes the magnet who attracts all and holds all tightly, making one big family. This happens only through the Love of the Guru. Without the Love of the Guru, where would you be? Elsewhere, no?

Bhagavan Shankar is saying, *Priyaṁ putradi yat prītyā tasmai śrī gurave namaḥ, Priyaṁ putradi yat prītyā*, which is like the love of the father and son. The parents always try to unite the family, they always try to keep the family together, no? Nowadays is different, but a true family is like this. Bhagavan Shankar is saying that the Guru is like the parent who unites the family together and brings all under one roof.

Verse 38

**Yena cetayate hīdaṁ
cittaṁ cetayate na yam
jāgrat svapna suṣuptyādi
tasmai śrī gurave namaḥ**

Salutations to the Guru, who enables the mind to perceive this world and Him the mind cannot perceive, who illumines the three states of the waking, dream and sleep.

Yena cetayate hīdaṁ cittaṁ cetayate na yam; here He says that the Guru enables the mind, enables each person to see the world, to enjoy the world, to be in this tangible reality. But yet, the mind can not perceive Him, which means, the Guru can't be perceived by limitation. Even if the mind wants to understand the Guru, it is impossible. Even the heart itself finds it difficult to perceive the Guru. The Guru is *jāgrat svapna suṣuptyādi*, enlightening the one who is in the waking state, active state. When you are dreaming, the Guru is there protecting you, and when you are in a deep state of samadhi, the Guru is there guarding, looking after you, so that you are not lost somewhere. So the Guru is not only here, visible in the outside. He gives the sadhana for you to do; in your meditation He is seated in front of you; and in your deep sadhana He is the eternal guide guiding you.

Verse 39

**Yasya jñānādidaṁ viśvaṁ
na dṛśyaṁ bhinna bhedata
Sadeka rūpa rūpāya
tasmai śrī gurave namaḥ**

Salutations to the Guru by whose Knowledge this creation is no longer seen as different from the Supreme Being Himself whose form is Truth.

So, in the form of Truth the Guru reveals that this creation is not just a void, this creation is not only emptiness. Here Bhagavan Shankar Himself is saying, that the creation is not just emptiness; nothing is empty, because everything is full of Narayana! And it is only through the Grace of the Guru, that one no longer perceives the emptiness, but the fullness. This means that the Supreme Being is present everywhere, at all times. So, there is no such thing as the void. The void is just a step to the Ultimate Supreme Reality.

In this verse Bhagavan Shankar, who is a great Advaita, is saying to Parvati that the Guru is the One by whose Knowledge one sees that the whole creation is no different from the Supreme Being.

Everything is the Ultimate Lord Himself. In each thing around you there is the Supreme Lord Himself infused into it; God is in each atom. So there is no emptiness, but there is only the Supreme Being. And here Bhagavan Shankar is saying that only through the Grace and the Knowledge given by the Guru, one will perceive that Reality, whose form is Truth.

Verse 40

Yasyāmataṁ tasya mataṁ
mataṁ yasya na veda saḥ
Ananya bhāva bhāvāya
tasmai śrī gurave namaḥ

Salutations to the Guru, who says he does not know Him, but not him who claims to know Him. The Guru is not different from the Supreme Being.

This is very funny, you see. *Yasyāmataṁ tasya mataṁ mataṁ yasya na veda saḥ*, here He is saying that the Guru limits Himself. He utilises Maya to hide His True Form, and He hides it so well that sometimes He Himself forgets about it! Because He plays the part of a human too much. He becomes more human than humans. No, He never forgets!

Mataṁ yasya na veda saḥ; "but not him who claims to know Him" - so here He says that those who think that they know the Guru, they don't know Him in reality. They just know what He wants them to know. But those who are humble, and deeply surrendered in their hearts, they don't see any difference. They know, not in the mind; they know in the core of their hearts that there is no difference between the Supreme Reality and the Guru. And those who know this Supreme Reality, they don't need to talk about it. They just need to surrender!

Verse 41

Yasya kāraṇa rūpasya
kārya rūpeṇa bhāti yat
kārya kāraṇa rūpāya
tasmai śrī gurave namaḥ

Salutations to the Guru who, though being the Primary Cause, is seen as an effect; who is both cause and effect.

Here Lord Shiva is explaining to Parvati that everything is due to the Grace of the Master. People remember in one life only what happens in their life, without realising that it is a long continuation of events. It is not just coincidentally, "Oh, you know, I woke up with my right foot and I found my Guru today." It is not a coincidence that God just decided to bring you on the spiritual path, or to place you in a certain lineage, to place you under the care of a certain Guru. It's a long relationship, which comes since the beginning of creation. From the mind one can only perceive this relationship in a limited way. Whereas in the Consciousness you will see that everything rotates, coming from the same primary Atom itself, which is the Lord Himself. From that on, everything started to split itself into parts. But the origin itself is from the beginning. That's why He said, *kārya rūpeṇa bhāti yat*; "the Primary Cause" of everything.

Verse 42

Nānā rūpamidaṁ sarvaṁ
na kenāpyasti bhinnatā
kārya kāraṇatā caiva
tasmai śrī gurave namaḥ

Salutations to the Guru who reveals the truth that this world of diversities is, in fact, undifferentiated and that it is merely a play of cause and effect.

Everywhere, wherever we go, whatever we do, we do it always for something. You love because there are some expectations behind it. You work because you have a certain aim: you want something. This duality of cause and effect co-exists because this is how the mind of man works. Whatever a man does, he does it for the result of it: you work to get money; you spend the money to get something; when you get that thing you wanted, you get unhappy; when it's finished you feel sad - so there is always cause and effect in everything. But here, He also says that to the one who is surrendered to the Guru's Feet, the Guru reveals that one is beyond that; you are not in the game of the outside; you are not in the game of the mind, but you are beyond that reality. You are in the True Self! And in your True Self, in your true aspect, you have control over the cause and effect.

It is not just merely saying, "Oh, you know, this happened just like that!" No. You see, from the beginning itself, what your actions are and what the result of them will be. And you can alter it if you feel that this will bring you happiness or misery. You don't just go into it and then you say, "Oh, damn!" No. You can see it before it happens, whether this will bring you misery or happiness.

Verse 43

**Yadaṅghri kamala dvandvaṁ
dvandva tāpa nivārakam
tārakaṁ sarvadā 'padbyaḥ
śrīguruṁ praṇamāmyaham**

Salutations to the Guru whose Lotus Feet eradicate the anguish of all dualities and help us cross misfortunes and calamities.

Here you see what I have just said: by surrendering to the Master, one is awakened to the state of Oneness by the Master Himself - the state of perceiving the Supreme Reality beyond the duality.

Tārakaṁ sarvadā 'padbyaḥ śrīguruṁ praṇamāmyaham explains that He is the One who helps us cross all misfortunes and calamities.

So misfortunes and calamities are due to the state of the mind. One makes oneself unhappy or happy. We always say that this is right and this is wrong. This is how one perceives things, how one sees things.

For example, I love this beautiful flower, okay? For me it's beautiful! But Chatur thinks, "A boring flower like that and He is calling it beautiful?!" But how do you see 'beauty'? Is it the outside beauty or the inner beauty? The same thing with misfortunes and calamities. How does one see those? How does one perceive them? Where do they come from? This is the Guru's role: to make you realise that, since the beginning, all that you perceive in the outside, it's not you. Once you can pierce the outside deeply and see the Ultimate Reality into it, then you will see that there are no misfortunes, there are no calamities.

So, salutations to the Guru, who removes this anguish, who removes this pain, because He shows you that this pain is self-inflicted; you bring it upon yourself and make yourself miserable, through the judgement, the constant judging - by seeing the duality of things.

Verse 44

Śive kruddhe gurustrātā
gurau kruddhe śivo na hi
Tasmāt sarva prayatnena
śrīguruṁ śaraṇaṁ vrajet

If Lord Shiva becomes angry the Guru can come to your rescue, but if the Guru becomes angry, even Shiva cannot save you. Therefore, make every effort and seek refuge in the Guru.

This is the most beautiful verse in the *Guru Gita*. Here Bhagavan Shankar Himself is saying that if He gets angry the Guru can rescue the person, but if the Guru becomes angry, even Shiva cannot save you. Therefore, make every effort and seek refuge in the Guru. This is the reality, not only in the *Skanda Purana* but also in the *Bhagavatam* Itself. Lord Narayana Himself described that if an arrow is shot, the Guru can divert that arrow. He will change its direction. So, here He said that if God gets angry the Guru can save you, because He is merciful. But if the Guru gets angry, even God cannot save you. Because it's through the Guru that you are perceiving God. So why would He save you if you have offended the Guru Himself? Only the Guru can save you at that moment.

This is shown clearly in the story of Durvasa and King Ambarisha. King Ambarisha was a great devotee of the Lord. He was eternally serving the Lord and on an *Ekadasi* day, he was fasting, so he couldn't even take one sip of water. There was an according time to break the fast, and Sage Durvasa came. Sage Durvasa was known for his anger. His anger was always sitting on the tip of his nose. Durvasa came to test the king and said, "I have come to have food with you. Prepare the food, I will just go to take my bath and then I will come back." But there was a specific time when the king had to break his fast. While the sage went to take his bath, the king was waiting and time was passing. The time for breaking the fast, to get the punya, to get the merit, was approaching, so everybody in the court said, "King, you have to break the fast now, to receive the punya of your sacrifice of the Ekadasi."

The king said, "How can I do that? I can't take anything before Sage Durvasa has eaten!" But yet, there is a correct time to break the fast, so they all thought about it and the elders said, "Okay, just take a sip of water!" The king said, "Okay, one sip of water is not much, like that the fast will also be broken and he will not know about it." King Ambarisha took a little bit of water and drank it. At that moment, Sage Durvasa entered and got really angry! He was burning red, like a tomato! Out of that burning anger, a ball of fire came out of his head and was going towards King Ambarisha. Of course, the king just surrendered to the Lord and said, "As the Lord wills it!" He just bowed down saying, "Om Namo

Narayanaya". As the ball of fire was approaching, the king said, "It's the Lord's wish! I surrender to Him!" At that moment, when the fire was coming to burn King Ambarisha, the Lord sent His *Sudarshana Chakra*. The Sudarshana Chakra stopped the fire and kept carrying on to chop the head of Sage Durvasa. Here Durvasa started to run away, with the Sudarshana Chakra behind, following him. He ran to *Brahma Loka*. Brahma was ready saying, "Ah, Sage Durvasa you are here!" The sage looked behind him saying, "I can't stand to praise you! The Sudarshana Chakra is behind me to kill me!" Brahma said, "I can't help you. Go!" He arrived at Shiva Loka and Shiva said, "Hi, Sage Durvasa how are you?" "Don't talk! If you can save me, save me, otherwise tell me what I have to do!" Shiva saw the Sudarshana behind him and said, "This is the Lord's *Leela*, the Lord's Maya, I can't do anything for you. Go to the Lord Himself, maybe He can save you!"

As he knew that he had offended the Lord, Sage Durvasa went to Devi and said, "Devi, please help me!" Devi said, "I can't help you! Go to Mahavishnu, go to Narayana! He is the only One that can help you! It is His Sudarshana!" Sage Durvasa arrived in front of Mahavishnu and said, "Please Lord save me! Your Sudarshana will chop my head off. Please forgive me and take your Sudarshana Chakra back!" The Lord answered him, "How can I forgive you? To forgive, you need to have a heart. I don't have My heart. My heart is with King Ambarisha.

My heart is with My devotee. Only he can forgive you!" Sage Durvasa ran back to King Ambarisha, fell down at the king's feet and asked for forgiveness, "I have offended you. You, as a great devotee of the Lord, who is completely surrendered to the Lord, please forgive me!" At that moment, King Ambarisha bowed down to the sage and said, "How can I forgive you? You are a sage! We live through your blessing! I am nothing! So you bless me!" When Sage Durvasa saw this humility of King Ambarisha, his ego, his pride was crushed! And when King Ambarisha received the blessing from the heart of Sage Durvasa, the Sudarshana Chakra went back to Mahavishnu."

This story has a deeper meaning. Why Durvasa, being such a great yogi, didn't recognise who King Ambarisha was? Even if in this story the Guru is not mentioned, yet there is a deeper meaning into it, because King Ambarisha in his former life was Durvasa's Guru. And the Guru-disciple relationship doesn't end. Sage Durvasa offended the lineage itself, the Parampara itself, from the previous lives. That's why the Lord enacted in this way, to bring Durvasa to the Feet of one of his Gurus. Even if he takes many different lives, the disciple has to always seek the blessing of the Master. That's why Lord Shiva said that if He becomes angry then the Guru can rescue one because this is the duty of the Guru. But if the Guru gets angry, even God will not be able to save you.

Verse 45

Vande guru pada dvandvaṁ
vāṅmanaścitta gocaram
Śveta rakta prabhābhinnaṁ śiva
śaktyātmakaṁ param

Salutations to the Feet of the Guru, which are invested with white and red lustre, representing Shiva and Shakti.

Here He says that the Guru has both qualities, white and red. White stands for the calmness and red stands for fire, anger. In this verse, Shiva is explaining that the Guru has both the qualities of Shiva and Shakti inside of Him but yet He is above them. He stands over them, even if sometimes He has to utilise these qualities to teach the people, the disciples.

Verse 46

Gukāraṁ ca guṇātītaṁ
rukāraṁ rūpavarjitam
Guṇātīta svarūpaṁ ca
yo dadyātsa guruḥ smṛtaḥ

The syllable 'Gu' denotes that which transcends all qualities, while 'Ru', that which transcends form. The Guru is One who makes one realise that which is beyond attribute and form.

Here again He is explaining the word 'Guru' saying, "The syllable 'Gu' denotes that which transcends all qualities." The syllable 'Gu' in the word 'Guru' shows that the Guru stands above all the qualities which the mind perceives or can understand. We don't see the qualities, we perceive the qualities. While 'Ru' transcends all the forms. 'Ru' stands for transcending all that can be seen. If we combine these two aspects, it means that the Guru is above the form and all the qualities, above what we can see and feel.

Because very often what people see and feel is due to the mind concept. If you love someone, you see that person completely in a different angle. So, the feeling and the seeing go together hand in hand. If you like somebody, for example, today you like Chatur! Even in his jungly way, in his sadhu-like style, you like him. Even if he is wild, you still like him. In one year's time, maybe he will tell you something which you don't like to hear; straight away, in less than one minute, that beautiful sadhu-like style, which you used to like will be smashed. What will it be? "How ugly you look! How terrible you look!" This shows how quickly the mind flickers. How quickly you change your mood and how you see others. Matajis, you know that very well, no? Very often you shift; one moment you are very joyful but the next moment without any reason you change to the other side. It's true! This is how it is, isn't it, Mira? *[Mira answers, "Very much so."]*

For one who is surrendered to the Guru's Feet, the Guru is the One who makes one realise that which is beyond these two attributes, the qualities and the form. If you don't rise above that, then you are stuck into it. That's why yesterday the priest was referring to Ardhanarishwari, no? *[Swamiji is referring to the Navaratri Celebrations 2014]* People are always stuck into this aspect of man or woman. But this is just the body! Don't forget that you are not this man, you are not this woman! You are above that, you are the Atma! In the *Shiva Purana*, Shiva said, "Until you master the Shiva and the Shakti, you can't be the Self." That's what Ardhanarishwari stands for.

Later on you will see that there are 36 tattvas. In one of the tattvas it says, "Become androgynous." It doesn't mean that now you go and operate yourself. No. It's not in the physical level, but in the mind level. You have to transcend both qualities and both forms. If the Guru teaches you only to be a human being or just to be happy, "Hi, hi, hi, ha, ha, ha!" *[Swamiji says this pretending to laugh of happiness]* That's not the way. You have to go above that! Because the *Atma Tattva* - that's who you are. And that's the Guru's duty - to make you rise above the duality. Because if you master only one aspect and ignore the other aspect, then you have not mastered anything!

Verse 47

Atrinetraḥ sarva sākṣī
acatur bāhuracyutaḥ
Acatur vadano brahmā
śrī guruḥ kathitaḥ priye

O Dear One! The Guru is Shiva, the witness of all, although He is without three eyes. He is Vishnu, although He is without four arms. He does not have four faces, yet He is Brahma. This is what the scriptures say.

"O Dear One! The Guru is Shiva, the witness of all, although He is without three eyes." Bhagavan Shankar is saying that the Guru is Shiva Himself as the great witness. However, even if Shiva is represented with three eyes, the Guru is not. Because the eyes are not in the outside, but are inside. The Guru sees deep into the heart of the disciple. That's why the Guru recognises who are His disciples, who are devotees, who are His people.

It's not plainly, that you go to a Guru and say, "I feel good about you today. Are you my Guru?" Of course everybody will tell you, "Yes. You are my disciple. Come! Come!" There are gurus like that.

But here He said that a True Shepherd knows which are His sheep. That's what Christ said, no? So the Guru has this *trinetra*. He has these eyes of wisdom, the eyes to perceive the deep relationship from a long lineage. Because it's not by coincidence that you come to the Feet of the Master. Like I said, it dates back a very, very, very long time.

Acatur bāhuracyutaḥ, the Guru is "Vishnu, although he is without four arms". The Guru is doing all these things even just by sitting in one place. He is always looking after the welfare of His devotees. Do you know how wonderful it is to sit in one place and see the world? You don't need to travel around. It's nice, I tell you!

The Guru does not have four faces, but yet He is Brahma. The Guru doesn't have these four faces as Brahma, which are looking in the four directions of the universe, yet He is Brahma Himself.

Śrī guruḥ kathitaḥ priye; that's what the scriptures talk about: how one has to love the Guru and surrender to Him. *Śrī guruḥ kathitaḥ priye*, so become the dear one of the Guru.

Verse 48

Ayaṁ mayāñjalirbaddho
dayā sāgara vṛddhaye
Yad anugrahato jantuś
citra saṁsāra muktibhāk

I bow down to the Guru, the ocean of mercy, with folded hands for His Grace, which delivers the soul from the world of dualities and diversity.

Here again He instructs one to surrender to the Feet of the Master. Know that the Master, however harsh the Master can be, however strict the Master can be, yet the Master is very merciful. Even in the strictness there is great mercy. With some people, due to their samskaras, the Guru has to be strict towards them; otherwise He will not lead them to where they have to be. So in that strictness, there is also the mercy, because by being strict they will be saved; if the Guru is not strict, they will damn themselves. So what do you think is better? The strictness, no?

And for some the Guru has to be smiling and calm, gentle, because they need it like that. But in the deepness the Guru is neither this nor that, He is beyond the dualities and diversities. It's just a game which the Lord Himself enacts through the Guru. But if one is truly surrendered, one will realise that, one will perceive that.

On the other hand, if one sees the Guru only from the outside perspective saying, "Oh my goodness! This Swami Vishwananda is an angry person." Then, they will not perceive what the Master is doing for them. Very often I see that children perceive more than the adults.

Verse 49

Śrīguroḥ paramaṁ rūpaṁ
vivekacakṣuṣo'mṛtam
Manda bhāgyā na paśyanti
andhāḥ sūryodayaṁ yathā

The Guru's supreme form is pure nectar to the eye of discrimination. Just as a blind man cannot see the sunrise, an unfortunate person cannot perceive the Guru's glory.

He said, "The Guru's supreme form is pure nectar to the eye of discrimination." The one who has viveka, who has True Knowledge, the one who has wisdom, perceives the Guru through the eye of discrimination. Discrimination here doesn't mean judgement but stands for True Knowledge. The one who is absorbed inwardly perceives the true form of the Master, not the physical form in the outside, but what is seated inside. One will realise that the Guru was, is and always will be.

The disciple reaches *Mokshadham*, *Vaikunta*, but the Guru, out of mercy, will always come. The Guru always chooses to be here until the last disciple, the last bhakta has entered Vaikunta. This is the Grace, the mercy of the Guru. Even if it doesn't happen in one life, it will happen in another life. The Guru will always make the way. Even if the Guru doesn't incarnate – because very often people think, "Okay, I can't do it in this life, I will do it next life. He will come again." The Guru doesn't need to come, he doesn't need to incarnate – if you incarnate 100 times, will the Guru incarnate 100 times for you? No. But from the Supreme, from the other higher dimension, the Guru will guide that person in that life.

Here it is very important to say that through the eyes of discrimination, one should see the Master not just merely as a person, but one should perceive the True Form of the Master. "Just as a blind man cannot see the sunrise, an unfortunate person cannot perceive the Guru's glory." In the second part of this verse He said that people who are so much into the material world, how would they perceive the True Form of the Guru, when their mind is rotating so much into the outside? These people will never perceive the deeper reality. They stay blind. Such is this blindness, if someone sees the Guru as a mere person. But when one's eyes are open, one will perceive the Master differently.

Verse 50

**Śrīnātha caraṇa dvandvaṁ
yasyāṁ diśi virājate
Tasyai diśe namaskuryād
bhatyā pratidinaṁ priye**

O Beloved, bow down in the direction of the Guru's Feet with devotion every day.

Here Bhagavan Shankar is saying that one should bow down to the Feet of the Master. However, to bow down to the Feet of the Master is not just, "Oh, because everybody is falling down, I shall bow down also." No. Bow down with reverence and love - it doesn't matter where you are!

If you have in your mind the intention of bowing down to the Master's Feet, from each corner of the world, wherever you are, the Master is connected with you. He's not bound by time or space, because Masters are above time and space. He is seated deep inside the core of your heart. And if you perceive the Guru seated in the core of your heart, you'll see that wherever you are, the Guru is with you. Here He instructs you to not just perceive it but to bow down to the Feet of the Master. Don't feel ashamed, because it is only by showing the respect to the Master, by showing that you are willing to surrender, that the Master will bless you.

Verse 51

Tasyai diṣe satatam añjalireṣa ārye
prakṣipyate mukharito madhupair budhaiśca
Jāgarti yatra bhagavān guru cakravartī
Viśvodaya pralayanāṭaka nityasākṣī

O Noble One! The wise and the learned always offer handfuls of fragrant flowers over which bumblebees hover humming, to the direction in which resides the Supreme Guru who is witness to the eternal play of the creation and dissolution of the universe.

"O Noble One! The wise and the learned always offer handfuls of fragrant flowers over which bumblebees hover humming". Here He is addressing Goddess Parvati as the 'Noble One' because She has all the noble qualities inside of Her. She is the Mother of the universe and She possesses all the Divine qualities.

The reference to 'the wise and the learned' doesn't only stand for what one reads or learns in books, but for the True Wisdom which you feel inside your heart. Here He said that the ones who are surrendered to the Feet of the Master, they are wise indeed! They know where they stand.

He also says, "Always offer handfuls of fragrant flowers over which bumblebees hover humming," which means when the bee sees a flower and recognises the nectar inside that flower, do you know the joy the bee feels? It feels ecstatic and very joyful! Here He is saying that as the bee is in joy hovering over the flower, perceiving the nectar inside - you should be the same, finding in the Guru that nectar! And you should drink joyfully as the bee enjoys the nectar from the flower.

Jāgarti yatra bhagavān guru cakravartī; here He says that you should offer handfuls of flowers turning towards the Guru, who is a witness to the game of life, who is a witness to the creation and dissolution of this universe and sustainer of this universe. This means that you should turn inwardly, looking at the Master inside of your heart and offer the gratitude, the flower of gratitude to Him. Offer the flower of loyalty to Him. Offer the flower of truthfulness to Him. Offer the flower of surrender to Him. Offer the flower of Love to Him. Offer the flower of dedication to Him.

Verse 52

Śrīnāthādi gurutrayaṁ gaṇapatiṁ pīṭha
trayaṁ bhairavaṁ
siddhaughaṁ batukatrayaṁ padayugaṁ
dūtīkramaṁ maṇḍalam
Vīrāndvyaṣṭa catuṣka ṣaṣṭi navakaṁ
vīrāvalī pañcakaṁ
śrīman mālini mantra rājasahitaṁ
vande guror maṇḍalam

Salutations to the assembly of the three Gurus - Sri Guru, Paramguru and Paraatpara Guru and all other deities of all the peethams, the eight bhairavas and groups of accomplished sages and seers along with the Sri Maalini Mantra

"Salutations to the court of the three Gurus" - in this verse Lord Shiva is praising the Guru who carries the lineage, carries the blessing. That's why He said, Sri Guru, Paramguru and Paraatpara Guru and then there is another one, who is called Paramesti Guru, which is not mentioned in this verse. So there are not only three Gurus, but four - the assembly of four Gurus. Here Lord Shiva only said three.

Sri Guru means the immediate teacher itself. Then comes Paraatpara Guru, the senior living Guru, who carries on the tradition. Then comes the Paramguru, the highest teacher of that lineage and finally you have

Paramesti Guru, who is the founder of that lineage, the one who had the knowledge to establish that lineage.

He said that surrendering to the Guru is not just to say that we belong to so and so tradition. No. It means that you are in a very old tradition also. Here you see how important it is to surrender to a Guru. A Guru is not just somebody who puts an orange robe on and sits around, saying that he is a Guru. Or likewise, putting on a beautiful sari and calling herself a Guru. No. It's a whole long tradition in and of itself.

Even if a Guru is born fully realised in a certain part of the world, he still has to go through a Guru Parampara. He has to find the lineage where he belongs to. For us Mahavatar Babaji has chosen the Sri Sampradaya, the Vaishnava lineage from the first Paramesti Guru, which is Sri Ramanuja Acharya. Of course, even though Vaishnavism was always there, he solidified it in a formal way.

"Salutations to the assembly of the three Gurus - Sri Guru. Paramguru and Paraatpara Guru and all other deities of all the peethams." Here '*peethams*' stand for the Sri Yantra. When you did the Sri Yantra course, you saw that we call the place here Shree Peetha Nilaya. Shree Peeth means the abode, the place; peetham means the place itself where the Lord Himself resides. Shree Peetha Nilaya is where the Goddess Mahalakshmi resides Herself. It is Her abode. He also said that inside the Guru there is the peetham where all the devas reside. He is the Meru Itself. The Sri Yantra Itself is the Guru. The eight bhairavas - each Devi has a bhairava, each Devi has a guardian, no? So here He said that all these guardians, all the eight bhairavas are in the Guru Himself.

The lineage of the Guru Parampara itself is very old; it comes from great rishis and great munis, great sages from ancient times. When we do the Sankalpa, we always say Bharadwaja Gotra. I don't know whether you have ever noticed it. The Bharadwaja Gotra comes from Rishi Bharadwaja and that is my lineage. Of course, because here you are all from Abrahamic lineages, you see it as being different. But by following me, automatically you fall under the Bharadwaja Gotra lineage and he adopts you also. When people don't know their lineage, they claim always Krishna Gotra, which means a lineage that comes from Lord Krishna.

By surrendering to the Guru you receive the blessing of the whole lineage flowing through you. You become a carrier. The blessing is not just a blessing - you are a carrier. You represent and become the blessing of the Master, the blessing of the Guru is with you. And know also that you have not just received a blessing from one Guru only, because when the Guru gives the blessing, you receive the blessing of all the sages and saints from that lineage. That's why when you do Atma Kriya Yoga, if you just do it plainly like that, it doesn't have any effect; but when you get the Shaktipat, it activates a different channel inside of you. And this channel is the Guru Parampara - the Grace and blessing of all the Gurus and sages, saints from that lineage flow from the Master to the disciple; or from the Master to the teacher, and from the teacher to the student.

Here Bhagavan Shankar is saying, "along with the Sri Maalini Mantra." Like I said before, the Guru is the Sri Yantra, the Sri Chakra. And in the Sri Chakra, as you have seen, there are thousands of bij mantras, which means that all the devas are present in the Sri Chakra. So each mantra, each bij mantra flows through the Guru - Bhagavan Shankar is saying that Maha Devi is fully represented in the Guru Himself. So as all the bij mantras are in the Sri Chakra, the Guru is the Sri Chakra, with the eight guardians, the eight directions and the Sri Maalini Mantra, which is the full Shodashakshari Mantra - this is the Guru Himself.

Verse 53

Abhyastaiḥ sakalaiḥ sudīrghamanilair
vyādhi pradair duṣkaraiḥ
prāṇāyāma śatair aneka karaṇair
duḥkhātmakair durjayaiḥ
Yasminnabhyudite vinaśyati balī
vāyuḥ svayāṁ tatkṣaṇāt
prāptuṁ tatsahajaṁ svabhāva maniśaṁ
sevadhvamekaṁ gurum

What is the use of practising all those hundreds of rounds of long and deep pranayama, which are strenuous, tedious, hard to master and likely to cause numerous diseases? Attain the spontaneous state in which the powerful prana becomes still of its own accord through constant devotion and service to the One Guru.

"What is the use of practising all those hundreds of rounds of long and deep pranayama." Here Bhagavan Shankar as the Lord of Yoga Himself is saying that if one is not surrendered to the Feet of the Master, the long and deep pranayama is useless. This means that if you don't have the proper blessing of the Satguru, all the sadhana that you do, all your long pranayama, becomes useless; according to this verse it's of no use.

"What is the use of practising all those hundreds of rounds of long and deep pranayama, which are strenuous, tedious, hard to master and likely to cause numerous diseases?" Here Bhagavan Shankar is saying that without the blessing of the Master even the pranayama which is always good for health will become the opposite. Whereas the one who is surrendered attains "the spontaneous state in which the powerful prana becomes still of its own accord through constant devotion and service to the One Guru." He said that one can practise very hard, lots of different sadhanas and it can be very difficult, very tough. But the one who is surrendered, for the one who has constant devotion and service to his Guru, everything is given on a golden plate.

There is this wonderful story. There was a fellow from India by the name of Deepak.

Deepak was a very learned person. Once he was going through the shastras and he read in the scriptures that for a *pativrata*, for a wife the husband is God... *[Swamiji stops talking and looks at the audience. Then He says, "Complete shock and silence! Look, the husband is asking the wife, 'What did he say?' And she answers, 'Nothing!...' Swamiji laughs and the audience burst out laughing]*

Deepak was reading that for a wife the husband is God! For a child, his/her parents are God, *maatru devo bhava, pitru devo bhava*. And for a student, a disciple, the Guru is Parabrahma. Here you have to understand, like I explained yesterday, *Guru mātā pitā Guru bandhu sākha sakshat Parabrahma*, means that when a disciple surrenders to the Master - here I am saying, "Surrender!" It's not about the ones who plainly just take a Master, but I am referring to the one who is fully surrendered (body, mind and spirit) to the Master - the Master becomes the father, the mother, everything! That's why here He also said that Guru is Parabrahma. He didn't use the word 'God', but referred to the Guru as the Ultimate.

So, Deepak was reading in the shastras, in the *Guru Gita*, that if one is surrendered to the Guru's Feet and offers seva to the Guru, there are no *tirthas*, holy places, pilgrimage places to attend; there is no fasting to be made; there are no *upvas*, which means that there aren't any complicated things to do. Then, he was thinking, "If one is surrendered and offers service to the Guru's Feet, there is no need to go for pilgrimages, there is no need to chant big, big mantras, there is no need to do any harsh practices. There is no need to fast - in fact there is no need for anything extra! Just service to the Master, service to the Guru will give everything!" So this played in his mind, "Why should I walk up and down, North to South India on pilgrimages if I can just surrender to the Feet and serve the Master?" So deep inside, of course, it was the Guru Himself calling him, who had placed this feeling inside of him - it doesn't just appear like that. Although he was reading the shastras, probably he had already read them many times. But until then this point had skipped his mind. So, why on that specific time and specific moment was this reacting inside of him? Why was this making a certain effect inside of him? It is not just plainly like that. When one has this deep longing for the Master it's because the Master is also longing for the disciple. It's both ways. So, here Deepakji had this deep feeling inside of him, "I have to look for my Guru!" And deep inside of him he knew where he had to go. His feeling was pulling him towards the Godavari river and he knew that there was an ashram, where Guru Vedadarya was living. Vedadarya was famous because he used to teach the *Vedas*, *Upanishads* and the shastras to his students.

Deepak approached Vedadarya, bowed down and requested him with folded hands and humility, "Please accept me as your disciple!" Of course the Guru didn't just say, "Okay. I like your approach." But he had seen that inside of him there was this willingness, there was this deep longing inside of him. It's like when you come and ask, "Swamiji I want you to be my Teacher." What do I say to you? I say, "What do you feel inside of you?" That feeling inside of you is the truth towards yourself. It's not just me telling you, "Yes, come!" And then, after one month you just pack your baggage and go. No. That feeling of belonging to somebody must be there. The feeling, "I belong to you. Please take me!"

Vedadarya saw deep inside of Deepak and recognised

him as one of his sheep. So the Guru accepted him. Due to his complete dedication, deep interest and devotion to his Guru, in short time he learned everything. He learned the shastras, the *Puranas*, the *Upanishads*, the *Vedas*, everything.

One day the Guru called Deepak and told him, "You have excelled due to your devotion. You have reached a very high level of education. Now you don't need to study anymore about all these things." Of course, now the Guru wanted to test him. It's not just to learn and say, "Ah yes, I am a very learned person. I know the shastras. I know how to chant all this, 'bla bla bla'" No. This is the book knowledge, nothing else! It's like if you learn mechanics by reading a book: you learn that this part is a bulb; that part is a sealer; that part is a cylinder; that part is this and that. You know it! Then they will put a motor in front of you. You will be able to dismantle it, because it is easy - there is a screw or a bolt that you can just unscrew or unbolt. Very easy! But then, reassemble it! If you try to reassemble it, you'll have spare parts left. Because you don't have practice.

His Guru also wanted to teach him. So Guru Vedadarya said to Deepak, "Son, in my past lives I have committed some sins and of course I have cleansed in this life most of the sins from the previous births. But there are two sins which I have committed, which are very terrifying and very hard to expiate. For that I have to go to

Kashi, to Varanasi, because doing penance in Varanasi makes the result of one's penance ten times stronger. So quickly it will be finished! When I reach Kashi, I will invoke these two sins upon me. Due to those sins, I will suffer tremendously for two years. I will have dreadful diseases like leprosy and my body will secrete blood and pus. My appearance will change, I will become ugly and blind. My nature will change and it will be terrible: from gentle I will become very harsh with a very angry mood. There will be no tolerance in me. I will be in a very pitiable state." Then Vedadarya asked Deepak, "Would you help me? Would you serve me in that state?" In the mind of Deepak there was only one thing - service to the Guru, nothing else! So he answered without thinking, "Yes! I will serve you. However you are, I will serve you!" The Guru tried to dissuade him, "Are you sure you want to do that? You are still young. Think about it twice. It will be terrible!" Deepak said, "No. The only thing for me is to serve you." Then Deepak had this great feeling inside of him and said, "Listen, Gurudev! As I am young, I will invoke your sins, take the illness upon me and I will get blind instead of you. You don't need to go through that." Of course Vedadarya said, "Oh son, listen! One is responsible for his own sins. Only the one who has committed the sin can experience the effect of it. So, it's not possible. But if you want to serve me, then you can serve me!" Deepak replied, "Gurudev, I accept what you said and I will serve you!" Thus, with deep reverence and deep love he accepted to serve his Guru even if he would get ugly, deformed, blind and harsh.

Deepak and his Guru reached Varanasi, Kashi. They arranged a place for them to stay. They had darshan of Lord Shiva, Vishwanath, and Annapurna in Varanasi and after that Vedadarya invoked the two sins of his previous birth upon him. As he explained before, his body started to change and to suffer severe diseases. He had no tolerance. He was very ugly and very harsh. Seeing this terrible condition of suffering of his Guru, Deepak would cry every day. He used to take care of his Guru: to wash his wounds, to clean the body, to clean the blood and pus which was coming out of him, to give him medicine, to bandage him. He used to clean him even when he was going to the toilet. But inside of him he had never had any thought or feeling like, "Oh my goodness! This is terrible!" No. He felt great sadness that his Guru had to go through that suffering. But he also felt great joy in serving his Guru! He considered himself privileged to serve his Guru even in that state. He used to go and beg for food every day to feed his Guru. His Guru would eat everything and then would blame him for not bringing enough food. His Guru was very harsh and used to shout at him for no reason.

Once when he was begging for food, Lord Shiva Himself appeared in front of him. Seeing this great devotion of Deepak, Lord Shiva was very pleased and told him, "Deepak, I am very pleased with your Guru-bhakti. Ask me for a boon. What do you want?" As in the mind of Deepak there was only his Guru, he said, "I don't want anything. I will go and ask my Guru first, then I will let You know." Deepak rushed to his Guru and asked, "Gurudev, I saw Lord Shiva. I will ask Him to heal you!" The Guru said, "No. Don't ask this! You don't need to ask Lord Shiva to heal me. So that's it!" The next day, Deepak went to the temple and prayed to Lord Shiva. Lord Shiva appeared in front of him but he didn't ask anything of Lord Shiva. Lord Shiva was very pleased.

After some days, Mahavishnu also appeared to him and said the same, "I am very pleased with your Guru-bhakti and I want to give you a boon. Ask me." Deepak asked one question to Mahavishnu, "I know that You are the 'Deva Di Dev', the Lord of lords, the Lord of the Universe, but in my life I have never chanted Your name, I have never praised You, I have never sang any glory of You. Why do You want to give me a boon?" Then Mahavishnu said to him, "You saw God in your Guru and you served him. As you have seen your Guru as God, there is no difference between Me and him. As you have seen Me inside of him, You have served Me. By serving your Guru, by surrendering to the Guru, you have been surrendering to Me, that's why I have come to you. And you have proved that there is no difference - you know, deep inside you, that there is no difference between God and Guru so I will fulfil all your wishes.

Ask!" Then Deepak asked one thing only, "Grant me that I can increase my Guru-bhakti." So, that's what he asked for: to have more and more devotion to his Guru and to have the opportunity to serve his Guru more and more. Mahavishnu was very pleased and blessed him.

When Deepak came back to the Guru, he was shocked to see the Guru completely healed, like nothing had happened. His body was full of wounds with pus and blood coming out from them, but when Deepak came back he was completely healed. Meanwhile the two years had passed. This test lasted for two years. The Guru was very pleased and told Deepak, "You have passed the test!" Vedadarya blessed Deepak and said, "You are a true disciple." This is the difference between a disciple and a devotee.

Verse 54

Svadeśikasyaiva śarīra cintanaṁ
Bhavedanantasya śivasya cintanam
Svadeśikasyaiva can nāma kīrtanaṁ
Bhavedanantasya śivasya kīrtanam

To contemplate the form of one's own Guru is to contemplate infinite Shiva. To chant the name of one's own Guru is to chant the name and glory of the infinite Shiva.

To contemplate the infinite Shiva is the same as to contempate Narayana Himself. "To chant the name of one's own Guru is to chant the name and glory of the Lord", Narayana Himself.

As in the story I told earlier, in which Shiva and Narayana appeared to Deepak, this verse explains the same - to chant, to contemplate, to meditate and to focus the mind on the Guru is the same as concentrating on Lords Shiva and Narayana. And to chant the Guru's name is the same as chanting the name of Narayana or Lord Shiva.

Here He didn't say that you should chant the name of other Gurus. Because if you chant the name of other Gurus and if you meditate on another Guru, you don't receive any benefit. That's what Lord Shiva emphasised by saying, *Svadeśikasyaiva*, which means 'which belongs to you', 'which is yours'. Here He said, "Don't meditate on another Guru." Why should you meditate and chant the name of another Guru other than your own? You don't belong to anybody else. You belong to your Guru! And if you belong to your Guru, you have to meditate on your Guru and chant the name of your Guru, bearing in the mind that when you are chanting the name of the Guru, it is equal to chanting the name of the Infinite Lord, the Trimurti - Brahma, Vishnu and Shiva.

Verse 55

Yatpāda reṇu kaṇikā
kāpi saṁsāra vāridheḥ
Setu bandhāyate nāthaṁ
deśikaṁ tamupāsmahe

I worship the Supreme Guru; the single particle of the dust of whose Feet forms a bridge to cross the ocean of family and the world.

"I worship the supreme Guru"; here the Supreme Guru is Narayana Himself. There is no difference between Narayana and the Guru. Bhagavan Shankar is saying that He worships the Supreme Guru who is Brahma, Vishnu and Shiva. He worships the Ultimate Guru who is Shriman Narayana. And in this verse, He says that the Guru Himself is Narayana.

"The single particle of the dust of whose Feet forms a bridge to cross the ocean of family and the world." This reminds me of the verse in the Bible, when Christ Himself said, "I have come to separate the father from the son and the mother from the daughter." In this verse Lord Shiva is saying the same, explaining that the single particle of the dust of the Feet of the Guru is the bridge between this world and the Divine. He said it's a bridge for someone to cross over the family and the world because people are so attached to the family and the world; one creates so many attachments that one binds oneself to many lives. Due to this attachment one becomes miserable, unhappy.

Here He said that one who finds shelter at the Feet of the Master, the dust of the Feet of the Master becomes the bridge to liberation. One is freed from attachment to the family and to the world.

Verse 56

**Yasmād anugrahaṁ labdhvā
mahadajñānamutsṛjet
Tasmai śrī deśikendrāya
namaśc ābhīṣṭa siddhaye**

I bow to the highest Guru for the attainment of the desired fruit. His Grace destroys mighty ignorance.

Here He says, "I bow to the highest Guru for the attainment of the desired fruit." So what is the 'desired fruit' of the soul? The desired fruit of the soul, of the Atma, is to reach the Paramatma, to attain the Ultimate. You have one desire of the mind and you have one desire of the heart, but the soul's desire nobody truly knows. Only by surrendering to the Feet of the Guru, the desire of the soul itself will get fulfilled. It's easy to fulfil the desire of the mind; it's easy to fulfil the desire of the heart, but it's very difficult to fulfil the desire of the soul. The desire of the soul is a desire which the mind doesn't perceive; it's a desire which the heart itself doesn't perceive - how would you fulfil it?

Mahadajñānamutsṛjet, which means 'that great desire', the greatest of all desires which is the soul's desire. The soul's desire, which a person of the world doesn't know about, doesn't perceive due to attachments. They are so anchored into the illusion that they don't perceive the soul's desire. But the Grace of the Guru destroys this ignorance.

Namaśc ābhīṣṭa siddhaye, it is only by the Grace, by the Guru's Kripa, that this ignorance of the outside is destroyed. And only then, the desired fruit of the soul is revealed, given and attained.

Verse 57

Pādābjaṁ sarva saṁsāra
dāvānala vināśakam
Brahmarandhre sitāmbhoja
madhyasthaṁ chandra maṇḍale

The Guru's Lotus Feet extinguish the raging fires of worldly existence. In the centre of the thousand-petalled Lotus is situated the Moon Circle in Brahmarandhra (on the crown of the head).

"The Guru's Lotus Feet extinguish the raging fires of worldly existence." Here He is saying that desires are like fire, because one desire always leads to another desire: you want a car; after the car you want a house; after a house you want a wife; after a wife you want a child; after a child you want a cow; after a cow you want a job and so on and so on.

Once a disciple said to his Guru, "I would like to go and have my own hermitage." He left the ashram of his Guru and built a small hut. As he had to look after himself, he started to have his body, mind and consciousness only focusing on the outside. He only had two dhotis. Every day he used to change his dhoti. He washed the dirty one and put it for drying on a stone. One day he noticed that there were some holes in the dhoti – the mice had eaten parts of his clothes. So he was thinking, "This is very bad!" So, to save his clothes he said, "Because the mice have eaten my clothes, I have to get a cat." He got a cat and, of course, to keep a cat, you have to feed it, no? So he got a cow to get milk for the cat. To keep the cow he needed a stable, so he built a stable. To feed the cow he had to get hay. So he had a little farm and from his hut he started building a little house. To look after the cow, the farm and the house he needed a wife. So he got a wife. To feed the wife he had to go and look for work.

After one year the Guru passed by and was enquiring, "I had a disciple living here in a hut. Has anyone seen him?" The Guru was asking the disciple himself. The disciple had a long beard and was in a terrible state, like a zombie. Of course, the disciple was ashamed to reveal himself. Then, he said, "Gurudev, it's me!" The Guru nearly fainted. He could not recognise his disciple. Then, the Guru said, "What happened to you, my dear?" Then the disciple said, "This was all due to a piece of cloth." Just to save a piece of his clothes. This is ignorance.

The Grace of the Guru destroys this ignorance for the one who is fully surrendered, for the one whose only one desire is as Deepakji was saying, "Guru Seva, nothing else!" Whereas the disciple of this last story, just for a piece of his clothes went through the "raging fires of worldly existence" to the extreme. If he would have surrendered to the Guru truly, if he would have stayed with the Guru then, *Pādābjaṁ sarvasaṁsāra* would not have attached to him. He would be free. Bhagavan Shankar is saying that the Guru's Feet "extinguish the raging fires of worldly existence".

"In the centre of the thousand-petalled lotus there is situated the Moon Circle in *Brahmarandhra* (on the crown of the head)" which is in the Sahasrara, in the middle of it, the Bindu. The Bindu itself is the Guru. Here Bhagavan Shankar is explaining to Devi that in the Sri Yantra, Sri Chakra, you have the thousand-petalled lotus, but the Bindu, which is in the middle point - this centre point is the Guru Himself.

Verse 58

Akathādi trirekhābje
sahasradala maṇḍale
Haṁsa pārśva trikoṇe ca
smaret tanmadhyagaṁ gurum

In the centre of the triangle, with the points 'a', 'ka', and 'tha', with Hamsa situated close to it, the Guru resides. Always remember Him.

The mandala of the Guru is the triangle, *'a', 'ka', 'tha'*, which is Brahma, Vishnu and Shiva and in the middle is where the Guru resides. And *Hamsa,* which is Parvati, symbolising knowledge, is situated at His side. So in the middle of the triangle, the Bindu is the Guru. Always remember Him in that way. The Guru is the centre of all.

Verse 59

Sakala bhuvana sṛṣṭiḥ
kalpitāśeṣapuṣṭiḥ
Nikhila nigama dṛṣṭiḥ
sampadāṁ vyartha dṛṣṭiḥ
Avaguṇa parimārṣṭis
tat padārthaika dṛṣṭiḥ
Bhava guṇa parameṣṭir
mokṣa mārgaika dṛṣṭiḥ

The Guru's Divine glance creates all the worlds, nourishes all things, and penetrates to the essence of all scriptures. It regards wealth as a trifle. It removes failings and defects. It remains focused on the Ultimate, and though giving rise to worldly qualities, is firmly set on the final goal of salvation.

"The Guru's Divine glance creates all the worlds" - here you see that the glance, the vision of the Guru, creates the world for a bhakta. It is through His glance itself that the Guru "nourishes all things, and penetrates to the essence of all scriptures." Bhagavan Shankar is saying that just the eyes of the Guru create the world for a bhakta, nourish him and give him the deep essence, the deepness of all scriptures. Just the eyes of the Guru, nothing else! This is like the mother turtle.

The mother turtle doesn't need to feed its little ones. Just by looking in the eyes of the mother, the little turtles feel full already. The scriptures talk about that: the Guru is like the mother turtle, who doesn't even need to feed the little one. Just by looking into the eyes, the Guru can impart everything! *Sarva dṛṣṭiḥ yam chāha Guroḥ mūrtim bhyo namaḥ*, which means that the form of the Guru, the eyes of the Guru can give everything! *Dṛṣṭiḥ* means that just by merely looking He can fulfil everything: the deepest desire, the deepest thing, He nourishes everything. He can give the whole knowledge, the essence of all knowledge just by a mere look.

"It regards wealth as a trifle. It removes failings and defects." Here in the eyes of the Master, the wealth of the outside doesn't mean anything, because these are all tangible things, these are all passing things; today is here, tomorrow is not here. So the Guru's eyes remove all this ignorance, which creates the fall of mankind, bringing all defects upon oneself. The eyes of the Master "remain focused on the Ultimate, and though giving rise to worldly qualities, is firmly set on the final goal of salvation." The eyes of the Master, even if they appear to be in the outside, their focus are always on the Ultimate. And the goal of the Master is always the salvation of his disciple. There is nothing else that concerns the Guru than the salvation, the freedom of His disciple.

Verse 60

Sakala bhuvana raṅga
sthāpanā stambhayaṣṭiḥ
Sakaruṇa rasa vṛṣṭis
tattva mālāsamaṣṭiḥ
Sakala samaya sṛṣṭiḥ
saccidānanda dṛṣṭir
Nivasatu mayi nityaṁ
śrī guror divyasṛṣṭiḥ

It is the principal pillar holding the stage of all the worlds. It showers the nectar of compassion. It is equal to the garland of the thirty-six tattvas. It creates all time. It is permeated by the true bliss of Consciousness. May this Divine glance of the Guru be always on me!

"It is the principal pillar" - the Guru is this pillar, the Guru is Adhishesh Himself, who is upholding on His hoods the entire world. The Guru is the One who showers compassion. That's why earlier in a former verse (verse 44), it says that if Shiva gets angry, the Guru can save you. But if the Guru gets angry, no one can save you. This is due to His compassion, because the Guru is the most compassionate! The Guru doesn't think of Himself, but always thinks about the welfare of His disciple. The Guru can live a very wonderful life, no? But why He has to sit with all His disciples? Why He has to sit with His people? Why He has to take time and be all the time with His people? Because His life is for the people. He is not concerned about Himself. Out of compassion He is concerned for the welfare of His disciples. He wants that His disciples are freed from this worldly existence. He wants that His disciples attain the Ultimate Reality. That's the concern of the Guru and this is due to the the nectar of compassion the Guru has. It is not just compassion, the compassion is full with nectar. It is the sweetest compassion!

Here it is said that it is equal to the garland of the thirty six *tattvas*. Tattva means 'that which is transcendental and immanent'. He is talking about the thirty-six tattvas which define the individual person, but at the same time the Guru, who is Godhead Himself. Bhagavan Krishna Himself said, "I am in the form of the Guru. The true seeker sees no difference between Me and the Guru." But the ones who see the difference, they are still in illusion.

From the first thirty-five tattvas, thirty tattvas stand for the material world, the individual world and the other five tattvas stand for the intelligence, bliss, will, knowledge and action. Finally, the thirty-sixth one stands for the Supreme Lord, Unique, All-pervading.

"It creates all time." The Guru, the Jagadguru, creates all time. The Guru is permeated by the true bliss of Consciousness. The Guru is not just in Consciousness, but is in the bliss of Consciousness. People, when they do their sadhana, they come only to one stage of consciousness, but the Guru is permanently absorbed into the Divine Consciousness, into the Supreme Consciousness, into the bliss of it. He is the Consciousness, but He is enjoying this bliss. Because bliss is here to be enjoyed. If one finds this blissful state inside of oneself, one will see that it's not just plainly sitting in bliss. No. In bliss you are enjoying yourself! The same when we are chanting the name of the Lord, when you are singing every night *[Swamiji is referring to the Navaratri Celebrations 2014]*, you are all in a blissful state. In that blissful state you are not just sitting in a very blissful state, thinking, "I am in bliss." *[Swamiji says this with an affected voice imitating someone sitting in meditation and being proud about it]* No. Here bliss means that you are expressing yourself, but your mind is not in action; what is in action is your consciousness, your awareness. And in that awareness, in that consciousness, you don't think about the outside world. When you are playing, dancing, chanting "Haribol!" or "Jai Ma!" – I don't think that at that moment you are thinking about anything else. Your mind is fully here. You are all in this state. Bhagavan Shankar is saying that the Guru, who is the Master of the thirty-six tattvas Himself, the Lord of the three worlds, He is completely enjoying and expressing this bliss of the consciousness.

May this divine glance of the Guru be always on each of us! Here Bhagavan Shankar is saying that just the eyes of the Guru possess all these qualities. As He said in a former verse (verse 55), "The dust of the Feet of the Guru is the bridge from this world to the spiritual world" and just a glance of the Guru makes one transcend this reality into the Divine Reality. And only then, through the concentration on the eyes of the Guru, the true bliss of Consciousness shall awake inside.

Verse 61

Agnī śuddha samaṁ tāta
jvālā paricakādhiyā
Mantra rājamimaṁ manye
harniśaṁ pātu mṛtyutaḥ

O Goddess! I hold that this king of mantras, 'Guru', being pure as (gold) refined in fire, and tested thoroughly from all the sides in the flames of reason, always protects one from death.

"O Goddess! I hold that this king of mantras," Which is the king of mantras? OM. Here Bhagavan Shankar is saying that the Guru's name is likewise the king of mantras. Whoever chants the Guru's name alone will find everything, will attain everything!

Jvālā paricakādhiyā means being pure as gold refined in fire. When you find gold it is filled with dirt. How is gold refined? When it is put through fire and melted completely; then the impurities are separated from the gold; then you obtain pure gold. Here Bhagavan Shankar is saying that the Guru is the One who refines the disciple. He is the refiner. He gives the sadhana to purify the disciple.

"And tested thoroughly from all the sides in the flames of reason, always protects one from death." Here Bhagavan Shankar is saying that the Guru is constantly around the disciple. He tests His disciple, so that one realises the eternity of oneself. Because without tests one will not be ready. If the gold doesn't go through fire, how would it be purified? It would still be gold, but it would not be pure. It attains its purity only when it goes through tests, and this test is the flame. So here He said that the Guru also tests the disciples from all sides through the flames of reason. And the aim of the Guru, the aim of testing the disciple is not for His personal gain, but it is always to save the disciple from falling.

Verse 62

Tadejati tannaijati
taddūre tatsamīpake
Tadantarasya sarvasya
tadu sarvasya bāhyataḥ

He (the Guru) moves and moves not; He is far as well as near, inside as well as outside everything.

Here He shows that there is no place where the Guru is not. Whether He moves or He doesn't move, He is ever-present! "He is far as well as near." The Guru can appear far away, but in reality He is the nearest. And for some He can appear very near, but yet He is far. So this means that you can see somebody very close to a Guru, but it doesn't mean that the physical closeness means much. The physical closeness is due to samskaras from the past. The Guru has to keep somebody close or somebody far away. That's what this verse says, *taddūre tatsamīpake*, "He is far as well as near". He is far for the mind, He is far to grasp, because one is looking at the Guru always into the outside, the mind rotates only into the outside, one sees only into the outside. If you look towards the outside, you will see the distance. But if you look with the consciousness, when you look inside of your heart you will see that the Guru is the dearest and the nearest one. Once you have perceived the Guru inside of you, you will perceive the Guru everywhere.

Verse 63

Ajo'hamajaro'haṁ ca
anādinidhana svayam
Avikāraś cidānanda
anīyān mahato mahān

(He realises): "I am unborn, ageless, established in My own Self. I am unchangeable, embodying the bliss of Consciousness, an atom larger than the cosmos."

The Guru is eternally in this realisation that He is "unborn, ageless, without beginning or end." The Guru is always established in the Divine Self within His own Self. Even if the Guru appears as taking birth and aging with time, in reality this is all the drama of life, the drama of the outside. The Guru in reality is without beginning or end.

Even if the Guru appears very much to be in the outside world, with His mind running left, right, jumping and dancing; in reality the Guru is always absorbed into His own True Self.

The Guru always knows that he is "unchangeable, embodying the bliss of Consciousness, an atom larger than the cosmos." The atom that science talks about is very small, but the Guru talks about the Cosmic Atom, *Narayana Tattva*, which is the Super Atom, in whom the whole Cosmos, the whole universe, is present inside. In an atom there is everything into it. Imagine your body - how many atoms are inside it? So, this universal Atom, *anīyān mahato mahān,* this Cosmic Atom, which made this whole universe, is the Guru Himself.

So even if one sees the changes of the outside, know that the universal consciousness, the blissful consciousness is never changed. The Guru is always absorbed into that and the Guru always sees Himself as this Divine Consciousness which is unchangeable.

Verse 64

Apūrvāṇāṁ paraṁ nityaṁ
svayañ jyotir nirāmayam
Virajaṁ paramākāśaṁ
dhruvam ānandamavyayam

That tattva or nature is beyond all primeval things, everlasting, self-luminous, taintless and completely pure; that is the supreme ether, immovable, blissful, imperishable.

The Guru Tattva, or nature, is beyond all primeval things, everlasting, self-luminous, taintless and completely pure. So the Guru here is referred to as everlasting because the Guru doesn't have a beginning or an end.

The Guru is self-luminous because He always shines the Cosmic Light of God. God doesn't have a beginning or end, He is the Ultimate, so the Light of the Ultimate is the Guru.

The Guru is not touched by any stains of the outside. The stains of the outside are only on the outside, but the Guru, who is always absorbed into the Divine Consciousness, who is the Supreme Himself, is not touched by them. He is completely pure, even if on the outside it appears differently. The white clothes that one wears can be stained on the outside; you can throw some colour on it, it will change colour; but the Guru is always into that pure state. Karma doesn't have any effect on the Guru. In the story of Deepak (commentary of verse 53), the Guru said, "I have still two sins to expiate, to finish from past lives." This was just a test for the disciple! The Guru is beyond that. The Guru is the Supreme Ether. That ether is present everywhere. There is no place where it is not present. It is "immovable, blissful, imperishable", while all the other elements are bound by limitation: fire has a limit; water can dry out; air can stop flowing; earth can change its ways - but ether is the primeval element of which everything came out of. So that's why here He said that the Guru is ether Himself. He doesn't go through changes. He doesn't go through variations.

Verse 65

Śrutiḥ pratyakṣa maitihyam anumānaś catuṣṭayam Yasya cā atmatapo veda deśikaṁ ca sadā smaret

Always remember the Guru. His spiritual power can be discerned through the four sources of knowledge - the Vedas, direct perception, sacred historical texts, and inference.

Nobody becomes a True Guru by learning it. Here Bhagavan Shankar is referring to the Real Guru, the Satguru, the Jagadguru. There are gurus - the worldly guru, like I said before, a normal teacher will also be called a guru in Hindi. But their knowledge is due to what they read through text.

Bhagavan Shankar says that a True Guru is a personification of the *Vedas*, He doesn't need to read the *Vedas*, because He Himself is the essence of the *Vedas*. And He has this direct perception. It's not because somebody else told Him that it has to be like this or like that. No. Because He Himself is the incarnation of the *Vedas*, He has all the scriptures inside of Him, all the knowledge, and He can tap into it at will, whenever He wants. So this is how the Satguru is.

Verse 66

Mananaṁ yadbhavaṁ kāryaṁ
tadvadāmi mahāmate
sādhutvaṁ ca mayā dṛṣṭvā
tvayi tiṣṭhati sāmpratam

O One with mighty reason, seeing that You are very receptive, I now tell You the theme on which one should always contemplate.

Bhagavan Shankar is addressing Goddess Parvati as "One with mighty reason". So in different verses, He has been addressing Her differently according to the different aspects of Herself. And He is saying that in this aspect there is no difference between Her and the Guru.

He said, "Seeing that you are very receptive, I see that you have this deep interest, you are very eager to know more. I now tell you the theme on which one should always contemplate."

Earlier Bhagavan Shankar was trying to get the attention of Devi, but seeing that Devi is very willing - here Devi doesn't represent only Parvati's form, but She is representing Prakriti, the creation, which means that She is the representative of each person, each devotee. Here Devi Parvati is representing the bhakta, the disciple.

Verse 6 /

**Akhaṇḍa maṇḍalākāraṁ
vyāptaṁ yena carācaram
Tatpadaṁ darṣitam yena
tasmai śrī gurave namaḥ**

Salutations to the Guru whose Feet reveal the Supreme Being that pervades this indivisible (cosmic) sphere of animate and inanimate creation.

In the previous verse, Lord Shiva said that He would tell Parvati on whom She should contemplate. Here He tells Her that She should contemplate on the Guru's Feet. "Salutations to the Guru whose Feet reveal the Supreme Being." Here He said that your contemplation, your focus, your eyes, your concentration should be fixed on the Feet of the Master alone. The Guru's Feet "reveal the Supreme Being that pervades this indivisible (cosmic) sphere of animate and inanimate creation."

Only by surrendering, by keeping your focus and by meditating on the Feet of the Master, the Supreme Reality, Shriman Narayana Himself, who is present in all things, animate or inanimate, can be revealed. It's only through the Grace of the Master that this Truth can be revealed. Without the Grace of the Master it's not possible.

Verse 68

**Sarva śruti śiroratna
virājita padāmbujaḥ
Vedāntāmbuja sūryo yas
tamai śrī gurave namaḥ**

Salutations to the Guru whose Lotus Feet are bedecked with the crest-jewels of the Vedas (the Mahavakyas- the Grand Proclamations). He is the Sun whose light opens up the lotus of Vedanta.

"Salutations to the Guru whose Lotus Feet are bedecked with the crest-jewels of the *Vedas* (the *Mahavakyas* the Grand Proclamations)." Here Bhagavan Shankar is saying that Narayana always has the chest jewel on Him, the *kausthuba*. The kausthuba is the essence of the *Vedas*. The Guru's Feet are like this chest jewel which has the essence of the *Vedas* in itself, and which is ready to be poured out upon the disciples when they are ready.

The Guru "is the Sun whose light opens up the Lotus of Vedanta." Here He said that the Feet of the Master is the Light which opens up the lotus. You know the lotus always stays closed. But with the first rays of the sun the lotus starts to open up. Have you ever seen that? The lotus always opens up when the first rays of the Sun shine upon it. But before that, it doesn't; it stays always closed. Here He said that until the Grace of the Guru is poured upon the disciple, one is always closed and in ignorance. But when the Light of Grace is poured upon the disciple, one rises above the duality. If a guru only teaches one to be into the duality, then he's a teacher. But the Guru who can reveal how to rise above the duality of things, that's a True Guru who can give the Grace to go beyond the duality of the mind. It is not just about finding outside happiness, but about aiming for an even higher happiness, the inner happiness, the true happiness.

Verse 69

Yasya smaraṇa mātreṇa
jñānam utpadyate svayam
Ya eva sarva samprāptis
tasmai śrī gurave namaḥ

Salutations to the Guru. By merely remembering Him, one receives spontaneous knowledge. By attaining Him, everything is attained.

Here Bhagavan Shankar is saying that just by remembering the Guru, the Satguru imparts knowledge to the disciple. There is no need to do a big ritual; there is no need to do a big pranayama - it happens spontaneously. The more you surrender, the more spontaneous this will be. It's like a flower; the more the Sun shines upon it, the more it will open up.

The more people stay in the darkness, away from the light, the more they are in the shadow. Yet the more people stand under the light, the more they are brightened.

"By attaining Him, everything is attained." If you attain the Guru, you have everything!

Verse 70

Caitanyaṁ śāśvataṁ śāntaṁ
vyomātītaṁ nirañjanam
Nāda bindu kalātītaṁ
tasmai śrī gurave namaḥ

Salutations to the Guru, who is Consciousness, peace and eternity. He transcends ether and is without stain. He is beyond nada (divine music), Bindu (blue spot) and kala (visions).

"Salutations to the Guru, who is Consciousness, peace and eternity." Here again you see the three qualities of the Trimurti, in the form of the Guru. The Guru is "consciousness, peace and eternity".

The Guru earlier was referred to as 'the ether' (verse 64), and in this verse "He transcends ether and is without stain." Bhagavan Shankar refers to the Guru as *nada*, the Cosmic sound. So the Guru is Himself the Cosmic sound OM. The Guru Himself is the Bindu, the centre point in the Sri Chakra. The Guru is Kala. Kala has two meanings: time and vision. So here He says, the Guru is the vision, the sound and the centre point.

Verse 71

Sthāvaraṁ jaṅgamaṁ caiva
tathā caiva carācaram
Vyāptaṁ yena jagat sarvaṁ
tasmai śrī gurave namaḥ

Salutations to the Guru. He pervades this entire universe, consisting of the movable and immovable, the animate and the inanimate.

"Salutations to the Guru. He pervades this entire universe," The Guru, even if He seems normal, the Satguru, He is the One who pervades this entire creation.

"Consisting of the movable and immovable, the animate

and the inanimate," the Satguru is not only for the living, the Satguru perceives the Supreme Lord equally in the movable and the immovable. For the Satguru it is the same.

In the life of Saint Dnyaneshwar there was once a great yogi who was passing by Alandi. People had heard about the greatness of Saint Dnyaneshwar. That yogi was very powerful and he had thousands of devotees. While he was passing by Alandi, he had heard of Saint Dnyaneshwar and he wanted to meet him. This yogi had mastery over all living things; he could control all living things by his will. As he had heard that Saint Dnyaneshwar had given the commentary and translated the *Bhagavad Gita* into Marathi to the local people, he wanted to meet him. However, this was also due to pride because he was very arrogant. So he asked some of his disciples to go and call Saint Dnyaneshwar. He was sitting with his brother and sister and he said, "No. If he needs me, tell him to come. Why should I go to him?" But it's true, no? If you need somebody, you can't expect that the person will come to you. If you need somebody, you should go to that person! So, Saint Dnyaneshwar said, "No. I don't need anything from him. I don't need to meet him, why should I go and meet him? If he wants me, then he should come to me!"

Of course, when the disciples took the answer to the guru, he became very furious! He was very angry, "How dare he?! He must be very proud for not coming to see me!" You see, this is the quality, when someone is very arrogant and proud, they perceive that, even in the saints. They perceive the saint as arrogant and proud due to their own pride and ego. They always project it on the Guru.

Saint Dnyaneshwar said, "No." The guru became furious and said, "If he doesn't come, I will kill everybody in this village." Not forgetting that he had the power over all living entities. So having such power over the entities, he could also at will kill everybody.

Of course, Saint Dnyaneshwar was a great bhakta, he was so dedicated to Lord Panduranga Vittala. Vittala was constantly inside of him. For Saint Dnyaneshwar everything was Vittala, everything was Krishna and he knew that this yogi was very proud, full of arrogance inside of him and this was due to ignorance. Because people acquire pride, not because they want to have it. Who likes pride? Nobody. But the one who has it, it's due to the ignorance, and Saint Dnyaneshwar knew that this was due to that ignorance. So, the only thing that could destroy this ignorance was to show superiority over him.

Saint Dnyaneshwar was sitting with his brother and sister on a wall when the disciples of that saint came and said, "Oh, you know, our guru will destroy, will kill everybody!" Saint Dnyaneshwar said, "Oh, my goodness! This guru is very much arrogant and very much proud." So how to destroy his pride? Saint Dnyaneshwar prayed to Vittala and asked Him, "Lord, You know what is best for each one. And You know how to humble each person. So I ask You, 'Please have mercy upon me!'" So, at that moment the wall on which they were sitting flew up in the sky and from far away started advancing towards that yogi. As this wall was approaching, the guru could see that something was flying, but he could not figure out what it was. So, as this approached him - was in front of him - he saw that Saint Dnyaneshwar, his brother and sister were sitting on the wall and the wall was flying. At that moment he realised that Saint Dnyaneshwar, who is a bhakta, was far more greater than him. At that moment his ego was shattered. He came down from his throne, bowed down to Saint Dnyaneshwar and started praising him saying, "How great you are! I have only mastered the living, but you have mastered the living and the non-living - the animated and the non-animated - so for that you are the Satguru!" This is the quality the Satguru has. Don't judge the Satguru being just a normal, mere human being. The Satguru doesn't show everything to the people. He shows only what they want to hear and what they want to see.

Verse 72

**Jñana śakti samārūḍha
stattvamālā vibhūṣitaḥ
Bhukti mukti pradātāyas
tasmai śrī gurave namaḥ**

Salutations to the Guru who firmly rides the power of knowledge, who is adorned with the necklace of the thirty-six tattvas and who grants worldly fulfilment as well as salvation.

"Salutations to the Guru who firmly rides the power of knowledge." The Guru is full of knowledge and He knows what to give, whom to give it to, how to act. He's like a parent, or it's like when you talk to a baby. When you talk to a baby, no matter how old you are, yet you lower yourself to the level of the baby to talk to the baby. And it's the same when you talk to an elderly person also. So in the same way, the Guru lowers Himself from whatever level He is to the level of the common people, for them to understand Him.

The Guru "is adorned with the necklace of the thirty-six tattvas," and He is the One "who grants worldly fulfilment as well as salvation." So the Guru 'wears' and masters the thirty-six tattvas, which make this world, which make human beings move, act... the first tattva is OM, then there is Krishna Tattva and so on. The Guru has full knowledge of these tattvas. And it is by the Grace of the Guru, that whoever is surrendered receives what is needed, not for their own pleasure but for their salvation.

Verse 73

Aneka janma samprāpta
sarva karma vidāhine
Svātma jñana prabhāveṇa
tasmai śrī gurave namaḥ

Salutations to the Guru who, by the power of Self-knowledge, can burn up all the karma acquired through countless lives.

The Guru is beyond karma. But due to His complete surrender to the Supreme and by realising the Supreme Self within His own Self, by this mere Realisation, all the karma of all the lives is burned; not for Him, but for the ones who are completely surrendered to the Him. Here He says that the Guru doesn't live for Himself. The Guru's life on Earth is to burn all the karmas of His disciples and free them.

Verse 74

Na guroradhikaṁ tattvaṁ
na guroradhikaṁ tapaḥ
Tattvaṁ jñānātparaṁ nāsti
tasmai śrī gurave namaḥ

There is no truth higher than the Guru, no austerity more purifying than serving Him, no realisation greater than His Tattva. Salutations to the Guru who makes this realisation possible!

"There is no truth higher than the Guru," there is nothing higher than the Guru; "...no austerity more purifying than serving Him," which means that there is no sadhana that can purify oneself more than serving the Guru. There is no higher mantra, yantra or tantra that can better save oneself than serving the Guru. Serving the Guru is far simpler and much easier.

There is "...no realisation greater than His Tattva." As the Guru is OM, there is no difference between the Guru Tattva, the qualities of the Guru, and the qualities of the Divine. There is no other realisation than realising that your Guru is what you are seeking for. If the devotees realise that what they are seeking for is the Grace of the Guru, the Guru's Kripa - in the Guru's Kripa they will achieve everything.

"Salutations to the Guru who makes this realisation possible!" By Padaseva, by serving the Master, one realises that one's aim is to surrender to the Master. Praises be to the Guru! Only He can give you that Realisation; He can give you that Grace if you deserve it.

Verse 75

Mannāthaḥ śrījagannātho
madgurus trijagadguruḥ
Mamātma sarva bhūtamā
tasmai śrī gurave namaḥ

My Lord is the Lord of the universe, my Guru, the teacher of the three worlds. My Self is the Self of all beings. Salutations to the Guru!

"My Lord is the Lord of the universe." Here He means Narayana.

"My Guru, the teacher of the three worlds." He is referring to the Trimurti: Brahma, Vishnu and Shiva.

"My Self is the Self of all beings." This is the Realisation, it is Devi.

So, the Guru is the personification of the Lord, the Teacher and the Self.

Verse 76

Dhyāna mūlaṁ guror mūtiḥ
pūjā mūlaṁ guroḥ padam
Mantra mūlaṁ guror vākyaṁ
mokṣa mūlaṁ guroḥ kṛpā

The root of meditation is the Guru's form; the root of worship is the Guru's Feet; the root of mantra is the Guru's word; the root of liberation is the Guru's Grace.

"The root of meditation is the Guru's form." Here Bhagavan Shankar is saying that the aim of meditation is not even to achieve Him, to achieve a state of perfection or a state of emptiness. He said, "No. Because in emptiness you will lose yourself. There is no such thing as emptiness! Because the Lord Himself pervades everything." Then how can there be emptiness? There can't be any emptiness! That's why He said that the root of meditation is the form of the Guru.

"The root of worship is the Guru's Feet..." If you know the Guru, you can interact with Him and your sole worship is only to His Feet! Whatever deity you are worshipping, you are worshipping only the Feet of the Master.

"The root of mantra is the Guru's word," gurorvākyaṁ, it

is the aadesh. Whatever the Guru says is the mantra for that person. The aadesh, the word: whatever comes out from the mouth of the Guru is the mantra.

"The root of liberation is the Guru's Grace." That means that liberation happens just by the Grace of the Master. Without the Grace of the Master, liberation is seen as being very far away.

In all traditions it is like this. Whether you are a Vaishnava, a Saivite, a Shakta, a Ganapatya, or Brahmana - in all traditions of Hinduism, and also in other religions - in ancient times they all used to say the same - it is only through the Guru's Kripa that one is saved and freed.

Of course, nowadays everybody says, "Oh, for what do we need a Guru?" But this is the delusion which people have created in the modern society. People throughout the world have forgotten how to truly surrender. Only when one takes shelter at the Feet of the Master, then one gets the knowledge of how to surrender.

For sure you have all heard about Krishnamurti. He was always saying, "You don't need a Guru." That was his philosophy. Once he visited Anandamayi Ma. Of course, he went there out of respect, but also out of pride. Anandamayi Ma asked him a question, "You are preaching to everybody that one should not follow a Guru. But tell me one thing - these people who are listening to you, what are they doing? Aren't they following your teaching? Aren't you feeling happy by telling them what they have to do? So, don't be a fool! You are acting as a Guru. So, if you are acting as a Guru, how can you tell somebody else, 'You should not have a Guru!'"

Verse 77

Gururādir anādiśca
guruḥ parama daivatam
Guroḥ parataraṁ nāsti
tasmai ṣrī gurave namaḥ

The Guru is without beginning and without end. He is the supreme deity. There is nothing higher than the Guru. Salutations to the Guru!

"The Guru is without beginning and without end. He is the supreme deity." If one is surrendered to the Guru, there is no need even to surrender to God. If one is surrendered to the Guru, there is no need to worship any other form or any other deities.

"There is nothing higher than the Guru. Salutations to the Guru!" If one can perceive that the Guru is God, then there is no need of having any other form. But as long as one doesn't perceive God in the form of the

Guru, then it is important to worship, to take aadesh, to listen to the Guru's word and worship whatever the Guru has advised one to do. Until that realisation appears, that the Guru and the Lord are One, follow the advice of worship.

Once... Vishwamohini?! *[Swamiji addresses Swamini Vishwamohini]* You were asked this question in Vrindavan, "Why to put Tulsi leaves at the Feet of the Guru?" You see, in the Vaishnava tradition Tulsi is offered only to the deity. But according to Bhagavan Krishna Himself, there is no difference between the Guru and Him.

However, everybody offers Tulsi leaves to the image of the Guru after His death. But if you can't perceive that the Supreme Lord is seated inside the Guru Himself, then why to offer Tusi leaves to His picture when He is dead? Do you think that when He was alive He was not One with the Supreme? And when He is dead, then He is One with the Supreme? If you think like this, then you are completely in ignorance.

But if you can perceive that the Guru is the embodiment of the Supreme Lord Himself, *guru parama daivatam*, that He is the Supreme deity; if you can perceive the Lord Krishna Himself in the form of the Guru - then this will become the higher form of Realisation.

Verse 78

Sapta sāgara paryanta
tīrtha snānādikaṁ phalam
Guror aṅghri payobindu
sahasrāmśe na durlabham

The merit [punya] gained through dips in all the holy waters of the seven seas fade when compared to that gained through sipping even a thousandth part of a drop of the water of the Guru's Feet.

Here Bhagavan Shankar is saying, "...holy waters of the seven seas..." - you see, we have seven holy rivers, no? And these seven holy rivers create a certain purification in oneself. So, each river purifies one chakra in oneself.

Bhagavan Shankar is saying that even if you take a sip, not one drop, but "a thousandth part of a drop" from the Charanamrita, from the water which has washed the Feet of the Master - this is more than taking a bath in the seven holy rivers itself. Just a thousandth part of a drop.

But for that you need to have the firm faith and belief! It's not just about saying, "Ah, I have just washed Swami's Feet. I am going to drink a whole glass of it." It's about the faith. This *Guru Gita* is only for the disciples who are fully surrendered. They will understand that. Whoever is fully surrendered will get the full benefit of what Lord Shiva is saying here. Without full belief and faith in the

Guru, this will not happen.

All what Shiva has said is not plainly like that, but there is a deep meaning inside of it. However, you will receive that only when you are completely surrendered.

Verse 79

Harau ruṣṭe gurustrātā
gurau ruṣṭe na kaścana
Tasmāt sarva prayatnena
śrī guruṁ śaraṇaṁ vrajet

If Shiva is angry, the Guru will protect you; but if the Guru is angry, no one can save you. Therefore, with all your efforts, seek refuge in him.

Here again (and also in verse 44) Vyasa is reminding one of this matter, because it is very important. Guru Aparadh can happen, and it is so subtle that it can happen automatically. Sometimes you don't even realise it.

And this doesn't mean that the Guru is angry and curses somebody, but this is the universal law itself. The moment someone offends a Guru, from the Cosmos, from the Cosmic Energy, there is a certain curse which automatically goes to that person.

To attain a body of a human being, you have done lots of penance, punyas; you have accumulated many good qualities from previous lives. That's why you have gotten a human body. But Guru Aparadh can reduce you back to the animal state, willingly or unwillingly. This has nothing to do with the Guru Himself. It's all due to your offence to the Guru. This Guru Aparadh makes the Cosmos, the Supreme Lord Narayana Himself, enact in that way. This curse will automatically degrade that person to a lower level, sometimes even worse than the animal level.

However, the Grace of the Guru can save and can raise back up again the one who is surrendered, when one has true remorse in the heart and sincerely asks for forgiveness. Due to that true remorse, the Guru, out of His mercy and compassion, can elevate the person back.

Verse 80

Gurureva jagatsarvaṁ
brahma viṣṇu śivātmakam
Guroḥ parataraṁ nāsti
tasmāt sampūjayed gurum

The Guru is, indeed, the whole universe. He comprises Brahma, Vishnu and Shiva in His Being. There is nothing higher than the Guru. Worship the Guru devotedly.

Here Bhagavan Shankar is saying that in the Guru there are Brahma, Vishnu and Shiva and that, "there is nothing higher than the Guru." Because Narayana Himself is in the Guru. So here He said, "Worship with devotion the Feet of the Master."

Verse 81

Jñanaṁ vijñāna sahitaṁ
labhyate gurubhaktitaḥ
Guroḥ parataraṁ nāsti
dhyeyo'sau gurumāgibhih

By devotion to the Guru, one obtains all knowledge and realisation. There is nothing higher or greater than the Guru. Therefore, the devotees of the Guru should meditate on Him.

"By devotion to the Guru, one obtains all knowledge and realisation. There is nothing higher or greater than the Guru." So constantly here Bhagavan Shankar is saying, "Guru is everything! He can give you knowledge. He can give you Realisation at will. He can give you all this, when you are ready!"

"Therefore, the devotees of the Guru should meditate on Him." *Guroḥ parataraṁ nāsti dhyeyo'sau gurumāgibhih*. Here He says that the only meditation for someone who is fully surrendered is at the Feet of the Master. The disciple should always meditate on the Guru's form, on His Feet.

Verse 82

Yasmāt parataraṁ nāsti
neti netīti vai śrutiḥ
Manasā vacasā caiva
nityam ārādhayed gurum

Constantly serve the Guru with mind and speech. There is nothing greater than Him. The Vedas describe Him as 'not this, not this.'

"Constantly serve the Guru with mind and speech." Here He said that your mind should not wander around. When you are surrendered to the Guru, your mind should be always focused on the Guru. And your speech, whatever you talk about, should not be vain talk, but should always be about the Master.

"There is nothing greater than Him. The *Vedas* describe Him as 'not this, not this.'" *Neti netīti vai śrutiḥ*, Here Bhagavan Shankar is saying that the *Vedas* describe the Guru saying, "He is not this, not this," because He is everything! One can't put any limit to the Guru.

People perceive the Guru with the limited mind, yet He is beyond that. Even the *Vedas* say that He is "not this, not this". Even if you say that you have understood the Guru, the Guru will make you perceive that you have not understood Him. Even if you think that you know the Guru, yet He will make you perceive that you don't know Him really. You know only what He wants you to see. You can perceive only what He wants you to perceive. He can make you think that you know Him, but in reality you don't know Him. That's a quality of a true Guru. When you think that you know Him, in the next moment, He will show you another aspect of Himself, which you don't know. When you think that you have already mastered that aspect, He will make another aspect. The Guru is like... *[someone in the audience says, 'chameleon']* No. The chameleon will only take the appearance of what you put it on. If you put the chameleon on the red, it will become red. But if you put the Guru on the red, He will become green. So one can't grasp the Guru with the mind, but with Love one can perceive a certain reality.

Verse 83

Guroḥ kṛpā prasādena
brahma viṣṇu sadāśivāḥ
Samarthāḥ pravhavādau ca
kevalaṁ gurusevayā

Even Brahma, Vishnu and Shiva acquired their cosmic potencies by the Guru's Grace. They attained all power only through service to the Guru.

Here He said that "even Brahma, Vishnu and Shiva acquired their cosmic potencies by the Guru's Grace." Brahma, Vishnu and Maheswara are unknown to the people. But their potencies are known only when the Guru reveals them to a disciple. Only then the disciple gets to know who Brahma is, who Vishnu is and who Shiva is. But before the Guru reveals these potencies to a disciple, they are unknown.

For sure when all of you were young - did you know about Brahma, Vishnu and Shiva? Did you know about Krishna? No, you didn't know. But after the Guru has taught you about them, then they all become alive inside of you. Now you know who Brahma is, who Vishnu is, who Shiva is, who Devi is, who Krishna is, and so on, no? Otherwise, you would not know. That's what this means - they "acquired their cosmic potencies by the Guru's Grace. They attained all power only through service to the Guru." So the ones who serve the Guru attain this knowledge. They receive the Grace of knowing, they receive this power of the Trimurti within them.

Verse 84

Deva kinnara gandharvāḥ
pitaro yakṣa cāraṇāḥ
Munayo'pi na jānanti
guru śuśrūṣaṇe vidhim

Gods, kinnaras, gandharvas, manes (ancestral spirits), yakshas, charanas (beings of different order) and even sages do not know the proper manner and method of serving the Guru.

The gods, the kinnaras, the gandharvas, the spirits, the yakshas, different beings of different orders, the sages, they "do not know the proper manner and method of serving the Guru." Here Bhagavan Shankar is saying that they don't know how to serve the Guru.

Why? Because all of them were created directly from Brahma. Due to that they don't have any knowledge of Guru-bhakti. They don't have any knowledge of how important a Guru is. They are bound only by their duty. Whereas human beings, due to their knowledge and the Grace of the Master, can achieve a very high level of spirituality, even higher than the demigods, higher than the kinnaras and the gandharvas.

Only the ones who know and worship the Guru, the ones who have Guru-bhakti, know what is the most important. Indra can't say, "Okay, today I will not do my duty." Imagine that Śurya Dev, Surya Narayan will say, "Today I will not shine!" Do you think he has that capacity? No. He doesn't have that capacity. The Sun has to shine! This is His duty! Indra's duty is to give rain. Kubera's duty is to give wealth. They can't say, "I don't like your face, so I will do it like this." No. They are not bound by that. Because these deities are created directly by Brahma. They don't have Guru-bhakti. Even if they have their Guru to advise them, He is just an adviser, nothing else. They always do whatever... *[Someone in the audience says, "Whatever they want." Swamiji then explains...]*... not whatever they want, but whatever is allocated to them due to their duty.

Here Bhagavan Shankar is at the same time praising the bhakta, praising the devotee who has surrendered to the Guru saying, "You people are more fortunate!

Because due to the service to the Guru's Feet, due to the service to the Master, you can achieve what the devas can't." You can reach Vaikunta. You can achieve the Lord's Lotus Feet, whereas the devas can't. Indra can't walk into Vaikunta and say, "Narayana, I want to talk to you!" Whereas a bhakta can.

Verse 85

Mahāhaṅkāra garveṇa
tapo vidyā balāvitāḥ
Saṁsāra kuharāvarte
ghaṭa yantre yathā ghaṭāḥ

Even those with self-discipline, learning and strength continue to revolve on the wheel of the world like pots on a potter's wheel, due to their ahankaara, inflated pride and conceit.

Bhagavan Shankar is saying that if one doesn't understand the service to the Guru, if one doesn't take shelter at the Feet of the Master, one can be a learned person, one can have great strength, power, but this is nothing! It will not lead them anywhere, because they are inflated with pride, ego. They are blinded by ignorance. And due to their ignorance, due to their pride, they can have lots of self-discipline, practice much sadhana, learn many things, they can be very powerful. But if they don't have the Guru's Kripa, all this is in vain. Because all this will act only on the physical level. What about when you die? It's finished! But the ones who have the Guru's Kripa, they have secured their future life.

Verse 86

Na muktā devagandharvāḥ
pitaro yakṣakinnarāḥ
Ṛsayaḥ sarva siddhāśca
gurusevā parāṅmukhāh

Even gods, gandharvas, manes (ancestral spirits), yakshas, kinnaras, seers and siddhas cannot attain liberation if they neglect service to the Guru.

Bhagavan Shankar is again saying that the "...gods, gandharvas, manes (ancestral spirits), yakshas, kinnaras, seers and siddhas..." usually don't realise the importance of serving the Guru. That's why they can't be liberated. They don't get liberation. They don't attain the Feet of the Lord. They don't attain Narayana Himself. They can be great siddhas, they can be great sages, they can be gods and so on, but for attaining liberation they have to serve the Guru, Guru seva, *gurusevā parāṅmukhāh*, is very important! To attain liberation one should not neglect the service to the Guru.

Verse 87

Dhyānaṁ ṣṛṇu mahādevi
sarvānanda pradāyakam
Sarva saukhyakaraṁ nityam
bhukti mukti vidhāyakam

O Supreme Goddess! Listen. Meditation on the Guru grants all joys, all pleasures, comforts and enjoyments and finally, salvation as well.

Bhagavan Shankar is addressing the Supreme Mother saying, "To whoever meditates on the Guru, You shower them with joy, happiness; You fulfil all their wishes, the comfort, the enjoyment. It is You who brings the salvation." He said that only by meditating on the Guru's Feet, the Supreme Mother bestows all the Grace upon the disciple.

Verse 88

Śrīmat parabrahma guruṁ smarāmi
śrīmat parabrahma guruṁ vadāmi
Śrīmat parabrahma guruṁ namāmi
śrīmat parabrahma guruṁ bhajāmi

I remember my Guru who is Parabrahman (the Transcendental Absolute); I praise my Guru who is Parabrahman; I bow to my Guru who is Parabrahman; I serve my Guru who is Parabrahman.

"I remember my Guru who is Parabrahman," Bhagavan Shankar is saying, "I remember my Guru who is the Ultimate Transcendental Absolute Godhead, Narayana Himself."

"I praise my Guru who is Parabrahman," I praise Him. I am constantly meditating upon Him and His praises are constantly on my lips.

"I bow to my Guru who is Parabrahman," I offer my salutations to Him who is the Supreme Lord Himself.

"I serve my Guru who is Parabrahman," and I serve Him.

Here He used the word 'Parabrahman'. Krishna Himself said, "I am Parabrahman."

This is the mantra which a bhakta, or somebody who is truly surrendered to the Feet of the Guru, should chant, first thing in the morning, even before going out from bed. By singing this mantra, one reminds oneself of who the Guru is.

Verse 89

Brahmānandaṁ paramasukhadaṁ
kevalaṁ jñāna mūrtim
dvandvātītaṁ gaganasadṛśaṁ
tattvamasyādilakṣyam
Ekaṁ nityaṁ vimalamacalaṁ
sarva dhīsākṣi bhūtaṁ
bhāvātītaṁ triguṇarahitaṁ sadguruṁ
taṁ namāmi

I bow to the Satguru, the embodiment of the bliss of the Absolute, the bestower of the highest joy. He is absolutely alone. He is knowledge personified. He is beyond duality, formless as the sky, the theme of the grand Vedantic proclamations such as "Thou art That!" He is One, eternal, and free from impurities. He is immovable, the witness of the intellects of all creatures. He is beyond change and becoming, beyond the three basic qualities (gunas).

Brahmānandaṁ paramasukhadaṁ kevalaṁ jñāna mūrtim; Here He says that only the Guru, only the Satguru is the embodiment of the Absolute bliss. He is the One that gives the highest joy, bliss. He is bound by nothing.

Even the *Vedas* proclaim Him, "Thou art That!", "He is One, eternal, and free from impurities." So the *Vedas* talk about the Guru, who Himself is the great witness beyond all creation, beyond the changes - because the mind is always changing, but the Guru is always in the awareness, in the Consciousness; He is not bound by the changes of the outside. Even if the disciple changes, going up and down, the Guru always dwells in a uniform state, because He has mastered the three gunas: sattva, rajas and tamas.

Verse 90

Nityaṁ śuddhaṁ nirābhāsaṁ
nirākāraṁ nirañjanam
Nityabodhaṁ cidānandaṁ
guruṁ brahma namāmyaham

I bow to the Guru who is Absolute, everlasting and pure. He is beyond perception, formless and without taint. He is ever-thinking, conscious and blissful.

Here is the meditation. Bhagavan Shankar bows to the

Guru, who is the Absolute. There is no one beyond the Guru. The Guru is seated into the Consciousness, and into the Consciousness He perceives everything; not only in His devotees, but everywhere. Even if He has a form, He is not limited to that form. He can tap into any forms and manifest Himself in many forms. He is not limited only to one aspect or one way. That's why I always say, "I always have my ways. If plan A doesn't work, there is always plan B. If plan B doesn't work, C will come. If C doesn't work, we create D. If D doesn't work, we create E, and so on." So, the Guru is not bound by the way people think.

Verse 91

Hṛdambuje karṇika madhya saṁsthe
siṁhāsane saṁsthita divyamūrtim
Dhyāyed guruṁ candra kalā prakāśaṁ
cit pustakābhīṣṭavaraṁ dadhānam

Meditate on the Divine form of the Guru who is seated on the throne in the centre of the heart lotus, who shines like the Moon, who bestows the desired boon and throws open the book of Consciousness.

The Guru is the centre of the heart chakra. And it is through His Grace that when one's heart is open, one feels calmness inside oneself. And this calmness, this bliss, this state is the Grace of the Master Himself who fulfils the wishes of His bhakta. Lord Shiva Himself says, "The Guru gives everything to His disciples, to the ones who are fully surrendered to Him."

Verse 92

Śvetāmbaraṁ śveta vilepa puṣpaṁ
muktā vibhūṣaṃ vibhūṣaṃ
muditaṁ dvinetram
Vāmāṅka pīṭha sthita divyaśaktim
mandasmitaṁ sāndra kṛpā nidhānam

The Guru is clad in white robes, anointed with white paste, bedecked with flowers and pearls. He radiates joy. The Divine Shakti is seated on the left thigh of this two-eyed God. His face is lit with a gentle smile. He is the ocean of Grace. Meditate on Him.

Śvetāmbaraṁ, the white robe here stands for purity, because the Guru is always in purity. The Guru is never tarnished by anything of the world.

The white paste symbolises that whatever He has, He

can also transfer it to His bhakta.

The flower and pearls stand for the strength and purity.

"He radiates joy." The joy which the Guru radiates is not just plain joy, that today is here and tomorrow is not here, but it's the eternal joy of the heart. When one recognises one's Guru, there is a different kind of joy which awakens within oneself and this joy is something eternal. Even if the bhakta doesn't feel the same joy all the time, due to their mind state, or due to where they are in the world, yet this joy that the soul felt when one meets one's Guru, this joy is eternal. It always stays within one's heart and whenever the mind of that bhakta is turned inwards into his heart, diving into there to meet the Guru, that same joy awakens itself again.

"The Divine Shakti is seated on the left thigh of this two-eyed God." Here Bhagavan Shankar is saying that the Divine Mother Herself is seated on the Guru's left side. In verse 87 He also said that the Supreme Mother is ever ready to fulfil the wishes of the one who is surrendered to the Guru.

The Guru's 'face is lit with a gentle smile'. Bhagavan Shankar Himself is saying that the Guru is not bored. The Guru always has a smile on His face. Krishna is also always smiling. Krishna is never with a gloomy face, like in a very miserable state. Even in the middle of the battlefield, when He was talking to Arjuna, He always had a smile on His face. Because He is always aware of what is coming ahead. That's why He smiles. So in the same way, the Guru always has a smile on His face, because the Guru is always ahead.

"He is the ocean of Grace. Meditate on Him." Here Bhagavan Shankar carried on saying that the Guru not only has Grace, but He is the ocean of Grace, which means that His Grace is endless.

Verse 93

Ānandamānanda karaṁ prasannaṁ
jñāna svarūpaṁ nijabodha yuktam
Yogīndra mīḍyaṁ bhava roga vaidyaṁ
ṣrīmadguruṁ nityamahaṁ namāmi

I always bow to the worshipful Guru who is bliss incarnate, who bestows happiness, whose face is radiant with joy. His essential nature is knowledge. He is aware of His True Self. He is the adorable Lord of the yogis, the physician who cures the malady of worldliness.

"I always bow to the worshipful Guru who is bliss incarnate, who bestows happiness, whose face is radiant with joy. His essential nature is knowledge. He is aware of His True Self." Here Bhagavan Shankar is saying that because the Guru is aware of who He is, He doesn't need to tell anybody who He is! He doesn't need to show anybody who He is! Because the Satguru is absorbed into His True nature, His True Self. All the qualities of the outside are just to remind one of who He is, but He is not touched by all this. This is just the appearance of the outside, but He is constantly immersed into His True Self, His True aspect.

The Guru "is the adorable Lord of the yogis, the physician who cures the malady of worldliness". The Guru is the greatest yogi Himself, the Maha Yogi, Yogi Raj and it is Him who can cure the illness, the sickness of this world.

There are different kinds of sicknesses. There are sicknesses due to some bacteria or some viruses, like Ebola. Satya Narayana Das calls it not Ebola, but Haribola, because it makes people reach Hari very quickly.

There are the illnesses of the mind, which are nowadays mostly common. Due to their mind state, people make themselves miserable and unhappy. Due to that mind's state one can't free oneself.

Then you also have a spiritual sickness. What is the spiritual sickness? Pride, ego and everything related to that. This sickness doesn't let oneself be free. Lord Shiva said that the Guru has the medicine for this sickness. He knows how to remove the ego, to cut it down. He knows how to destroy this pride of His devotees. And when one doesn't have this, one is free.

Verse 94

Yasmin sṛṣṭi sthiti dhvaṁsa
nigrahānugrahātmakam
Kṛtyaṁ pañcavidhaṁ śaśvad
bhāsate taṁ namāmyaham

I bow to the Guru in whom shine all the five eternal cosmic processes - creation, sustenance, dissolution, control and award of grace.

The work of the Trimurti is in the Guru. He is Brahma, He creates. He is Vishnu, He sustains and He is Shiva, He destroys. He is the One who controls and is the One who gives the Grace to the ones who deserve it, in the form of Narayana. The Guru has mastery over creation, preservation, destruction; control over the matters, control over the pride and ego, control over the mind. That's why the Guru can give the mantra. Mantra can't be given just like that to anybody. Only when one is ready, one receives the mantra. Why the Guru gives the mantra? This means that the Guru has seen something, somewhere inside that person, which makes that person qualified to chant that mantra. The Guru Mantra will automatically act as a catalyst to control the mind, so that one is purified and made ready to receive the Grace. Because if you are not ready, what would you do with the Grace? Put it in a pot and put the pot on the shelf. No. It would be of no use. It would stay dormant.

Verse 95

Prātaḥ śirasi śuklābje
dvinetraṁ dvibujaṁ gurum
Varābhaya yutaṁ śantaṁ
smarettaṁ nāma pūrvaka

Remember the Guru and His Name every morning. This two-eyed and two-armed peaceful God is seated in the white lotus inside the Sahasrara chakra, with the gesture of assuring the boon of fearlessness.

"Remember the Guru and His name every morning." Earlier in the *Guru Gita* there was the mantra (verse 88):
Śrīmat parabrahma guruṁ smarāmi
Śrīmat parabrahma guruṃ vadāmi
Śrīmat parabrahma guruṁ namāmi
Śrīmat parabrahma guruṁ bhajāmi

Here He said that one should remember the Guru first thing in the morning. The moment the eyes are open, on your bed or on the ground, wherever you sleep, the first thing that you should remember the moment you are conscious of being awake, is the Guru. And the first thing that you should do in the morning is to recite the Name of the Guru.

The Guru, "this two-eyed and two-armed peaceful God is seated in the white lotus inside the Sahasrara chakra, with the gesture of assuring the boon of fearlessness", Abhayahasta. Lord Shiva carries on explaining to Goddess Parvati that the Guru is the One who is seated in the crown chakra, in the Sahasrara.

Earlier there was also a verse which said that one should see the Guru as Devi; there is no difference between them. As the Sahasrara, the crown chakra, is always represented as Maha Devi, Vishnu Maya - here Bhagavan Shankar is saying that it is the Guru Himself, the two-eyed God and two-armed, who is seated in the white lotus of thousand petals and it is Him who gives the boon of fearlessness. Therefore the ones who are surrendered to the Guru always have the hand of the Guru on them. And they should not fear anything. Knowing that the Guru is always with you, why should you fear something? If you have such trust and such dedication - if you have full faith in your Guru, you should not worry about anything else.

Verse 96

Na guroradhikaṁ na guroradhikaṁ
na guroradhikaṁ na guroradhikaṁ
Śivaśāsanataḥ śivaśāsanataḥ
śivaśāsanataḥ śivaśāsanataḥ

There is nothing higher than the Guru. Shiva is primeval. Shiva is primeval.

There is no one higher than the Guru. Even if Shiva is primeval, the Consciousness is primeval, but yet "there is nothing higher than the Guru". Here Bhagavan Shankar Himself is saying, "

Śivaśāsanataḥ śivaśāsanataḥ śivaśāsanataḥ śivaśāsanataḥ [Swamiji seems to have seen something and says, "Jagadambe Mata Ki! Hey Bhavani! So, even Maha Bhagavati Herself agrees with that!"] He said, "Shiva is primeval." But the Guru is higher than Him. The Guru is higher than the Consciousness. Because Shiva is the Consciousness only, but the Guru is the one who reveals the Consciousness!

Verse 97

Idameva śivaṁ tvidameva śivaṁ
tvidameva śivaṁ tvidameva śivam
Mama śāsanato mama śāsanato
mama śāsanato mama śāsanataḥ

Service to the Guru alone is beneficial. (The Guru is Shiva) This is My word.

There is no prayer. There is no word. There is nothing greater than "Service to the Guru". Here Bhagavan Shankar said, "This is My word". This is My word. This is My word. He said that through service to the Guru one will attain everything, but service to the pride will bring one's own downfall.

There is this beautiful story of Kabirdasji. Kabir is considered to be also an incarnation of Krishna Himself. Do you know Kabirji? He was a great bhakta of Sri Ram.

Kabir lived in the city of Varanasi, Kashi, where there was a great saint by the name of Ramananda. Ramananda was a great devotee of Lord Rama and his ashram was well-known; everybody knew that he was a great saint. Kabir wanted so much to be a disciple of Ramananda, because he knew that Ramananda was his Guru. As Kabir grew up in a Muslim family, whenever he would approach the ashram, the disciples of Sri Ramananda would get angry and push him away. But, Kabir wanted to go inside so much that he used to sit in front of the door and would not move. You see, Kabirji was actually never born. Kabir was found on a lotus by a Muslim couple. They were childless - similar to Shirdi Sai - they found him inside the lotus and then they brought him up. And for him also, there was no difference: he was always chanting the name of Ram; he was always praising Allah and Ram. The same. Because the name of God is One. God is One.

Kabirji had mentally accepted Ramananda as his Guru. Kabir had this eagerness, he had this deep devotion, so every day he would make a must to go to the door of the ashram, once or twice a day to try at least to see his Guru. Sometimes he would beg the inmates of the ashram, "Please, at least tell Gurudev that I wanted to meet him!" If he could meet him, even once in his life, that would be enough. He didn't want anything else. He just wanted to have Guru Diksha of Ramananda. But, they would push him away and sometimes they would beat him up. You know, at that time the Hindus were very dogmatic and wouldn't allow other castes or religions to enter the Hindu places. Today it's still like this.

As a great devotee of Lord Rama, Ramananda had a deep connection with Him. Once he had a mental vision of Rama and in that vision he saw Rama and Lakshman talking to each another. Rama was saying to Lakshman, "Let's leave this ashram and go away from here. Let's move out! Why should we stay here, when a true bhakta is being pushed away?" Because, you know, the Lord Himself dwells in the heart of the bhakta. Lakshman, who was generally quick-tempered said, "Let's leave this ashram right away! Let us not waste our time here! What are we doing in a place where a sincere devotee is being thrown out?"

When Ramananda saw that the deity, his beloved Rama was going to leave the ashram, he said, "Please Lord, don't leave this servant of yours! I am totally unaware of that happening in this ashram. Please tell me where I failed!" Then Lord Rama told him, "One of My devotees is longing to be initiated into my Divine name! He came to your ashram, every single day, and your disciples pushed him away. He has such bhakti inside of him! He just wanted to have a glimpse of you and receive the mantra from you, nothing else!" So, receiving the Guru Mantra is very, very, very, very important. Even Kabir, who was a great soul, an incarnation of the Lord Himself, longed for the initiation into the Guru Mantra.

When Ramananda heard about this occurrence in the ashram, he was shocked and promised to Lord Rama that he would look into that issue immediately. Then he asked Lord Rama, "Please give me a chance to correct my mistake and do not leave this slave of yours." Sri Ram agreed to stay in Ramananda's ashram, but under one condition: his bhakta Kabirdas should not be driven away from the ashram.

As soon as Sri Ramananda came back to himself, he told his disciples what had happened with Sri Ramaji. The disciples felt embarrassed and confessed that every day a Muslim did come to have darshan of Gurudev, but they pushed him away thinking that Sri Ramananda would not be pleased to meet a Muslim.

Ramananda had a deep pain inside of his heart, because he had given True Knowledge to his disciples. Yet what have they done? They have done the opposite, thinking that they knew better. So Ramananda could not sleep all night. On the other side, Kabir could not sleep either. Kabir was lying down on the steps leading to the bank of the Ganges crying intensely saying, "Why can't I meet my Guru? Why can't I receive the Divine Grace of the Holy Name from Him? Oh Lord Rama, another day has passed and I have not received Your Divine Name. I have not even had the Grace of seeing my Guru. When will I have the fortune of having Darshan of my Gurudev and receive aadesh from Him, receive the Diksha from Him?"

As Ramananda could not sleep, he decided to go for ablution in the Ganges. It was early morning and it was dark everywhere. Ramananda walked to the bank of the Ganges with a heavy heart and in a reflective mood. As he was going towards the Ganges, his sandal, his paduka touched the head of someone lying on the step. You know, whenever a saint steps on something, the first thing they do is to chant, to call the name of God, no? Ramananda always had "Ram, Ram, Ram" in his mind, so when his paduka touched the body of Kabir, he said, "Ram, Ram, Ram" straight away. At that moment, Kabir held the Feet of the Master, crying profusely. The touch of the Feet of the Master to Kabir; he was so much into that Divine ecstasy, that longing for his Gurudev that the touch of the paduka itself revealed that Sri Ramananda was his Guru. At that moment he got Guru Diksha and Guru Mantra directly from his Guru. The energy current flew from the paduka of Ramananda to Kabir and when the Guru said, "Ram, Ram, Ram" he received the mantra 'Ram' as the Guru Mantra. There was tremendous rejoicing in the heart of Kabir when he looked up at his Guru and said, "You have not just given the Guru Mantra in the ears only, like a Guru formally does, but you blessed me even with your paduka. You have stepped over me. You have touched me with it! How fortunate I am indeed!" Kabirdasji was in such an ecstasy, chanting the name of "Ram, Ram, Ram", dancing and crying out of joy that Ramananda felt deeply moved with his devotion and love. This shows that when people are really surrendered to the Guru, they feel a great bhav inside of them. Not just a plain bhav, but they have this great joy which Lord Shiva has been talking about in the *Guru Gita*. It's an eternal joy which comes from deep within one's heart.

There is this writing of Kabirji which says, "If I have the chance to see both God and my Guru at the same time, I would worship my Guru before I prostrate to God. Guru is like a mother. The mother takes care of the child from the day she conceives it. She puts up with lots of difficulties and sacrifices her desires for the welfare of the child. My Guru took me into His arms and fondled me when I was called a sinner by the rest of the world just as a mother would fondle her child. But God turned to look at me only after I was purified by the Grace and Love of my Guru just as a father would cherish and see his grown up child holding a high position in society and shares none of the difficulties of the mother." Kabir praised his Guru with such wonderful praises!

Guru Govind dovo khade, kaake laagav paay

balihari Guru aapne, Govind deeyo bataaye

"To whom shall I take refuge? To the Feet of God or to the Feet of the Guru? Because without the Guru's Grace I would never know God, but with the Guru's Grace I know God. So for me my Guru is my God." That's what Kabirji said.

So, hearing the story of Kabirdasji, one should remind oneself of the importance of the Guru Mantra. The blessing that the Guru Mantra carries. Because it is not just a mantra to please you, because it is fancy or because it's a trend to come and ask for the Guru Mantra. And, then you go and chant it loud and do whatever you want with it.

There is another verse that says that the Guru Mantra is more precious than any jewel and one should guard the Guru Mantra more than one's own life itself. This is how much importance one should give to the Guru Mantra, and how much responsibility one should take when one was given the Guru Mantra. It is one of the most important Grace once can receive. That's why this year I decided not to give a Guru Mantra to anybody anymore. Because people often don't know how important it is to receive the Guru Mantra. So the ones who have the Guru Mantra, lucky you! Because for the ones who have not received the Guru Mantra yet, they will also receive it, but first they have to chant Om Namo Narayanaya for twelve years; 16 malas of Om Namo Narayanaya every day for twelve years. Only then you can ask for the Guru Mantra...afterwards. Well, if I am still around.

Verse 98

**Evaṁ vidhaṁ guruṁ dhyātvā
jñānam utpadyate svayam
Tat sadguru prasādena
mukto'hamiti bhāvayet**

By meditating on the Guru in this manner, one automatically gains Knowledge. By the Grace of the Satguru one realises: "I am liberated."

"By meditating on the Guru in this manner, one automatically gains Knowledge." Here Bhagavan Shankar is saying that service to the Guru is the meditation to attain the Grace of True Knowledge, not book knowledge, but inner Knowledge. And this inner Knowledge is given only "by the Grace of the Satguru". And when one has the Grace of the Satguru, one realises oneself, one attains liberation and one attains the Lotus Feet of Shriman Narayana Himself. And this happens automatically. There is no formal initiation, but it happens through the dedication which the bhakta has. The more they are dedicated, the faster it happens.

The Guru will never go around telling you what you have to do all the time. You also have to take the responsibility of surrendering yourself to the Feet of the Master. Otherwise one can do sadhana for years and years and years, yet still doesn't receive anything. Whereas for the one who is completely surrendered, in a fraction of a second the Guru can give everything. No. Even a fraction of a second is too much! In the verse 78, Bhagavan Shankar Himself said that the Guru can give everything in just a thousandth part of a drop of the Charanamrita. Like this, the Guru can give Realisation instantly. And the Grace of the Guru flows automatically from Him to His disciple. It doesn't matter where He is, what He is doing, in which place of the world the disciple is. The moment they have complete *Shraddha*, faith and surrender to the Master, the Grace flows from the Master to the disciple. Here I'm utilising a disciple, because in this verse Bhagavan Shankar talks only about a disciple, not about a devotee.

Verse 99

Guru darśita māgeṇa
manaḥ śuddhiṁ tu kārayet
Anityaṁ khaṇḍayet sarvaṁ
yat kiñcidātma gocaram

Purify your mind by following the Guru's path. Detach yourself from all transient things perceived by the mind and senses.

"Purify your mind by following the Guru's path." Here He said that once you have taken shelter to the Guru's

Feet, a second thought should not be in the mind. The mind has to be fixed and cemented. Your mind should not wander around saying, "Have I done the right thing? Is He really the true Guru, the right Guru?"... and whatever, whatever... if there is any doubt in your mind, that means that you are not ready to surrender to the Feet of the Master. And with such doubt it will not lead you anywhere. But if you have fixed your mind at the Feet of the Master, if you have fixed your mind to the path of following your Guru, don't let any second thought awaken inside of your mind.

"Detach yourself from all transient things perceived by the mind and senses." Here He said, in the second part of the verse, *anityaṁ khaṇḍayet sarvaṁ yat kiñcidātma gocaram* - detach yourself, detach the mind, don't let the mind be fixed on side thoughts, second thinking. Don't let the mind run towards the outside. Don't let the mind be drawn towards what the others say. But detach from these things which are transient, which are not permanent. Fix your mind strongly at the Feet of the Guru, by whose Grace you will receive the Ultimate and the permanent things.

Verse 100

**Jñeyaṁ sarva svarūpaṁ ca
jñānaṁ ca mana ucyate
Jñānaṁ jñeyasamaṁ kuryān
nānyaḥ panthā dvitīyakaḥ**

The essential goal of all is the object of knowledge, while the mind is the subject. Realise the identity of the subject and the object. There is no other way to salvation.

"The essential goal of all is the object of knowledge, while the mind is the subject." True Knowledge is beyond the mind. True Knowledge is wisdom. The mind is just there to act. If you have True Knowledge, if you are truly aware, then the mind is under your control. But if you don't have True Knowledge, then the mind controls you and makes you dance to its tune. Then the mind is always jumping around like a monkey, from one tree to the other, from one thought to the other, from one desire to the other; then you will never be free. One is never free. One becomes very unsettled and very restless.

But when the mind has True Knowledge, like Lord Krishna said in the *Gita* (Chapter 6, verse 5), "A mind which is controlled is your best friend, but the mind which is uncontrolled is your worst enemy. Be aware of such a mind." Bhagavan Krishna Himself said that you must have Guru-bhakti! You must have this Knowledge of surrendering to the Lotus Feet of the Master to purify the mind. To lower the mind by bowing down to the Lotus Feet of the Master; then humility is awakened. And when humility is awakened, you automatically become humble. And when you are humble, pride doesn't find its place. But if you are very proud, the mind itself makes one become very proud. The mind itself makes one arrogant and ignorant.

Jñānaṁ jñeyasamaṁ kuryān - "Realise the identity of the subject and the object." The mind is the subject and is always running towards the object.

"There is no other way to salvation," so if you have True Knowledge, you have full control of the mind. If you have the control of the mind, you will know that you should not dwell on to outside. If you have the True Knowledge of the Self, you know that you have to dwell within your heart.

Verse 101

Evaṁ śrutvā mahādevi
gurunindāṁ karoti yaḥ
Sa yāti narakaṁ ghoraṁ
yāvaccandra divākarau

O Supreme Goddess! He, who speaks ill of the Guru in spite of hearing all this, falls into the most dreadful hell and rots there as long as the Sun and the Moon last.

"O Supreme Goddess!" Here Bhagavan Shankar is addressing Maha Devi as the Supreme Goddess, Maha Shakti Yogamaya.

Here it's a warning, "He, who speaks ill of the Guru in spite of hearing all this, falls into the most dreadful hell." Shiva Himself is saying, "If you hear all this that I am saying right now, yet you speak ill of your Guru, you think ill of your Guru, you will fall in the worst hell." Not just hell, but the worst one. As the Guru can give you the highest state itself, in the same way, the Guru Aparadh can make you fall deeper than hell.

Maybe somebody will commit a sin and goes to a certain hell. There is not only one hell. There are many hells. Like there are many heavens, there are also many hells. If somebody commits a crime, they will go to one kind of hell for a short holiday, like Bhagavan Krishna said in the *Gita*. Then after that, you are born again to expiate the sin you had committed.

Bhagavan Shankar is saying that the ones who offend their Guru, who speak ill of their Guru will go to "the most dreadful hell", which means they go to rot in the most terrible hell. "...as long as the Sun and the Moon last," which means for a very long time. They shall be in that hell "...as long as the Sun and the Moon..." shine.

There was once a saint who offended his Guru. He was a saint himself but he offended his Guru, so when he died he went to the lowest hell, the most terrible one. It is said that he was there for thousands of years. Due to that offence it was meant for him to be there forever, but when he was there, he felt sincere remorse and was constantly thinking about how he would amend himself. In that state, during these thousands of years while he was there, he was always meditating on the Gurudev's form and chanting his Gurudev's Name, nothing else. So by the Guru's Grace, the Guru went there, took him out, freed him and elevated him even to a higher degree of surrender, because even when he was in hell, he was constantly thinking of his Gurudev.

Similar to the story of Adam and Eve - by offending God, as God is the Supreme Guru, they were in hell for thousands and thousands of years until Christ Himself went there to uplift them, to take them out and free them. Such is the state of the one who speaks ill of one's Guru in spite of hearing all this. Here Bhagavan Shankar, Lord Shiva Himself, is saying, if you have the great blessing - Grace - the great opportunity of hearing the *Guru Gita*, but you still offend your Guru, it is the worst, because through receiving this knowledge you know that you should not. But if one still does that, after receiving, after hearing what Lord Shiva Himself has been saying, then one will be punished.

Verse 102

Yāvat kalpāntako dehas
tāvadeva guruṁ smaret
Gurulopo na kartavyaḥ
svacchando yadi vā bhavet

Continue to remember the Guru until the end of time, as long as the body lasts. Never disobey the Guru, even on attaining spiritual freedom.

"Continue to remember the Guru until the end of time, as long as the body lasts," continue constantly remembering, chanting and meditating on the Guru until your last breath.

"Never disobey the Guru, even on attaining spiritual freedom," *Gurulopo na kartavyaḥ*, always follow what the Master asks and never disobey, even if you are free one day, even if you attain liberation. Even if you have attained freedom, Mukti, the Guru always stays the Guru. You will never go above the Guru. And if you think that you will go above the Guru, you are completely mistaken. And automatically, as you have reached freedom, it can also be removed.

Verse 103

Huṅkāreṇa na vaktavyaṁ
prāñaiḥ śiṣyaiḥ kathañcana
Guroragre na vaktavyam
asatyaṁ ca kadācana

A discreet disciple should never speak discourteously or utter lies before the Guru.

A direct disciple, a true disciple, someone who has truly surrendered "...should never speak discourteously or utter lies before the Guru." Bhagavan Shankar is saying that if one who is surrendered to the Guru, and yet when the Guru asks something, one lies about it, one will also bear the punishment.

Here Bhagavan Shankar is saying, "A true disciple, a true bhakta, should never speak any lie in front of the Guru."

Verse 104

Guruṁ tvaṅ kṛtya huṅ kṛtya
guruṁ nirjitya vādataḥ
Araṇye nirjale deśe
sa bhaved brahma rākṣasaḥ

One who talks to the Guru rudely, argues irreverently and speaks in insulting terms, would be reborn as a demon in a waterless jungle.

"One who talks to the Guru rudely, argues irreverently and speaks in insulting terms, would be reborn as a demon in a waterless jungle," which means, in the desert. The one who speaks rudely to the Guru, argues, who doesn't show any respect, insults by any means, they will fall to such a degree that they will be born as entities, demons, even lower than animals. They will be born as demons not among the people, but in places where there is nobody. Because these demons, they always find great joy in harassing people, no? But here Bhagavan Shankar, who is also the Lord of all the demons, said, "I shall banish the one who rudely argues or speaks insulting their Guru. I shall banish them in a place where there will be no one to harass. So they will not even find joy in harassing or giving trouble to people." Terrible, huh?

Verse 105

Munibhiḥ pannagairvā'pi
surairvā śāpito yadi
Kāla mṛtyu bhayādvāpi
gurū rakṣati pārvati

O Parvati! The Guru can offer protection from curses pronounced by sages, serpents, and gods and also from the fear of death.

Here Shankar Bhagavan is explaining, "O Parvati! The Guru..." who is merciful, compassionate, full of Love, can always offer protection. The Guru whose heart is full of Love, True Love, will protect from the curses, will protect from the curses pronounced by the sages, the nagas, the "gods and also from the fear of death." So, here He was reminding of how compassionate the Guru is, how loving the Guru is. Even if someone offends Him, He is the only one who can stop that curse. He is the only one who can, out of Love for His bhakta, give full protection and save the one who has offended Him.

This reminds me of the story of St. Parthenios. Once, he had one disciple. This disciple was a former sailor and was very rude and very harsh. He stayed in the monastery of St. Parthenios in Chios for some time. Of course, at the beginning he was very attentive and very joyful, but after sometime he became very restless and didn't have any patience to follow what St. Parthenios asked from him. Once St. Parthenios told him to do something. He got very angry with St. Parthenios and what did he do? He slapped St. Parthenios. St. Parthenios was very old at that time, so he fell down. As he realised what he had done, he ran away towards the harbour. St. Parthenios' monastery is in the mountain, so from the mountain he ran down to the town of Chios. When St. Parthenios came back to himself, he started to cry for his disciple. He went down, looking for him everywhere. And he was crying, wondering where he could find his disciple, even after he had slapped him, after he had offended him. How merciful he was! How much love he had for his disciple that he went to look for him. When he found him - of course the sailor thought that St. Parthenios was coming to shout at him, so he started running away. But as he was running away, St. Parthenios started running behind him saying, "Please don't run away from me!" Then the sailor stop and said, "What do you want from me, old man? It was not enough that I slapped you?" At that moment, St. Parthenios fell down on his knees in front of him and said to him, "I beg you, please! Return back to the monastery." As the sailor was looking at St. Parthenios, he felt so bad in his heart, he felt great remorse inside of him, seeing how much humility his teacher had, that he himself was falling down in front of him and asking him to come back to the monastery. That moment made a great change inside of him, so he decided to come back to the monastery, fell down to St.

Parthenios and asked him, "Please forgive me!"

Of course St. Parthenios didn't want that his disciple would fall in the deepest hell, so he forgave him. Over the next few days, the disciple of St. Parthenios was very dedicated and he had again achieved this love inside of him, even higher than what he used to have before. Then, after three days, he passed away. St. Parthenios knew that he would die soon after committing a great sin. And due to that sin it would be thousands and thousands of years in hell before he could expiate it. Thus, in order to save him from that, St. Parthenios took it upon himself and protected him. So, this is how the Master takes upon himself to protect the disciple and the devotees.

Verse 106

**Aśaktāhi surādyāśca
aśaktā munayas tathā
Guruśāpena te śighraṁ
kṣayaṁ yānti na saṁśayaḥ**

Even gods and sages cannot save one who has been cursed by the Guru. Such a wretch undoubtedly perishes.

Here He said that if the Guru curses someone... not directly - the Guru Himself will not curse someone. Because the Guru is full of Love. How can He curse? The Guru doesn't curse anybody directly, but if one has attained the Guru Aparadh and has been cursed by the Cosmic Guru Himself, like I explained earlier (commentary of verse 79) - if one offends the Guru, automatically the curse will come to that person from the Cosmic Lord Himself who is the Supreme Guru, the Guru in the form of the Cosmic Lord. And when someone has been cursed by doing Guru Aparadh, even the gods can't save that person. Even the sages, the rishis can't save that person. Only the Guru Himself can save.

Shiva Himself said, "I Myself can't save anybody who has been cursed by the Guru. But the compassionate Guru, He can save the person" (verses 44 and 79).

"Such a wretch undoubtedly perishes," Here He said

that if one has attained the Guru Aparadh and the Guru Himself had cursed his disciple, for sure with full guarantee that one will perish.

Verse 107

Mantra rājamidaṁ devi
gurur ityakśara dvayam
Smṛti vedārtha vākyena guruḥ
sākṣātparaṁ padam

O Goddess! Among the words of the Srutis and the Smritis, the two-syllables 'Guru' is the mightiest mantra, which leads to the highest state.

Among all the mantras, the only two words 'Gu' and 'Ru' are the mightiest mantra. If one chants the name of the Guru, one receives the highest state of spirituality. One attains liberation. One attains the Lord Himself and dwells with the Lord eternally. So here He said, "Chant the name of the Guru and be free! Meditate upon the Guru and attain His Grace."

Verse 108

Śruti smṛtī avijñāya
kevalaṁ gurusevakāḥ
Te vai sannyāsinaḥ proktā
itare veṣadhāriṇaḥ

Though ignorant of scriptures, a faithful servant of the Guru is a true sannyasin, a monk. Others are mere pretenders, donning robes, which they do not deserve.

Here Bhagavan Shankar is saying that it's not the robe that one wears, that makes one a true devotee, a true Brahmachari or a true Swami. It's not the robe, but the faith that they have in the Guru. It's about how much they are surrendered to the Guru, how much love they have for the Guru. Even if they don't have any knowledge of the scriptures, but if they are surrendered to the Guru, they are considered higher than the learned ones, higher than the ones who are wearing a certain colour of clothes or who have taken certain vows - because if one is not surrendered, one doesn't deserve it. But the one who serves the Guru, the one who is surrendered to the Guru is truly a true bhakta, a true *sannyasin*, a true Brahmachari, just by the service to the Guru.

Verse 109

Nityaṁ brahma nirākāraṁ
nirguṇaṁ bodhayet param
Sarvaṁ brahma nirābhāsaṁ
dīpo dīpāntaraṁ yathā

Just as one lamp lights another, the Guru imparts to the disciple awareness of the Absolute Being who is eternal, imperceptible and without form or attribute.

You see here, the state in which the Guru dwells: the Guru dwells in the Absolute Reality, the Guru dwells in Narayana Himself, who is with form and without form. The Guru dwells in that awareness of the Absolute Being. The Guru is aware of His eternity. And the Guru can transfer that, just like a lamp lighting another lamp, the Guru can give, can impart that same awareness to the one who is fully surrendered.

Verse 110

**Guroḥ kṛpā prasādena
ātmārāmaṁ nirīkśayet
Anena gurumāgeṇa
svātmajñānaṁ pravartate**

By the Guru's Grace the disciple should meditate on the Supreme. The path shown by the Guru leads to Self-Realisation.

Here He said, only when one receives the Grace of the Master, one should meditate on the Ultimate Reality. Without that blessing, without the order from the Master, one should not adventure into the deep forest which one can't handle. "The path shown by the Guru leads to Self-Realisation." If people enter the forest by themselves without the proper instruction from the Guru, for sure they will be lost. But with the proper instruction and order from the Master, the Guru's Grace can make the Supreme easily attainable.

Verse 111

Ābrahma stamba paryantaṁ
paramātma svarūpakam
sthāvaraṁ jaṅgamaṁ caiva
praṇamāmi jaganmayam

I bow to the Guru who encompasses the entire universe, who is the Supreme Being permeating all things and creatures, movable and immovable, from Brahma to a blade of grass.

Here He said that the Guru, the Cosmic Guru, the Guru's True form is everywhere. The Guru's True form is Shriman Narayana Himself, the Supreme Being. This Shriman Narayana, who is present in each atom, each molecule, is only the Guru Himself. "From Brahma to a blade of grass," which means, from Brahma to the smallest thing. For the bhakta it should be only the Guru, nothing else.

Verse 112

Vande'haṁ saccidānandaṁ
bhedātitaṁ sadā gurum
Nityaṁ pūrṇaṁ nirākaraṁ
nirguṇaṁ svātma saṁsthitam

I always bow to the Guru who is Existence, Consciousness, and Bliss; who transcends all distinctions, who is everlasting, perfect, without form or attributes; and who is rooted in His own Self.

Bhagavan Shankar is saying that the Guru is not just what one sees with the eyes. Even if the Guru appears human, the Guru is Satchidananda. The Guru is Eternal Bliss, Consciousness and Existence.

He transcends all distinctions. The Guru is not bound by the limitation which even He portrays sometimes. The Guru is not bound by the limitation of what one sees in the outside, but He is everlasting. He is above that what one can see and perceive. Even if He is not here, in the physical body, He is everlasting.

And whatever the Guru does, even if to the mind something appears not to be perfect on the outside, it is fully perfect. That's what Bhagavan Krishna Himself said in the *Gita*, "If someone follows Me, even if they do something which appears terrible on the outside, they must be considered saints. Because I dwell in them constantly, and they dwell in Me. They just do what I command them to do. Because they are surrendered to Me, I am surrendered to them. So I use them to act into the world. But in reality they are fully absorbed in My perfection." That's what Bhagavan Krishna Himself said in the *Gita*. So the Guru is always centred within His own Self, rooted in the Supreme Lord, Bhagavan Krishna Himself inside of Him. The Guru knows no difference.

Verse 113

Parāt parataraṁ dhyeyaṁ
nityam ānanda kārakam
Hṛdyākāśa madhyasthaṁ
ṣuddha sphaṭika sannibham

The Guru is beyond all beyonds, the highest object of meditation. He is the eternal bestower of happiness. He resides in the centre of the heart - pure and bright as a crystal.

"The Guru is beyond all beyonds, the highest object of meditation." So the Guru is beyond everything which one thinks is the limit. He is beyond that limit which one perceives. If one thinks that liberation is the Ultimate, the Guru is above liberation itself.

"He is the eternal bestower of happiness. He resides in the centre of the heart - pure and bright as a crystal." So the Guru who is seated inside the heart is ever-pure and full with brightness. He is the one who showers happiness and joy on His bhakta. That's why Bhagavan Shankar said that He is the highest object of meditation.

Verse 114

**Sphaṭika pratimā rupaṁ
dṛśyate darpaṇe yathā
Tathātmani cidākāram
ānandaṁ so'hamityut**

Just as an image of crystal shines in a mirror, similarly that which is Consciousness and Bliss, the True Self, shines in the buddhi (knowledge).

As one can see the multicolour light emanating from a crystal, the mirror reflects that light thousands of times and repels it back to the crystal, and it reflects it back again. When you take a crystal, and the crystal has the light shining on it, you perceive only one light. But when you put that crystal in front of a mirror, that light is multiplied much more. Here He said that similarly the Consciousness, the Bliss, the True Self shines ten times more when it is near to the Guru. The Guru is like the mirror: He amplifies that shininess. He amplifies those qualities of oneself. If one comes with a gloomy face to the Guru, that will also be amplified until one realises that one should not be in that state and should awake oneself.

Verse 115

Aṅguṣṭha mātra puruṣaṁ
dhyāyataścinmayaṁ hṛdi
Tatra sphurati bhāvo yaḥ
śṛṇu taṁ kathayāmyaham

Now I shall speak to you of the inner state, which arises when one meditates on the thumb-sized, Conscious Being dwelling in the Heart.

Here Bhagavan Shankar is saying that even if your meditation is just that much ("thumb-sized") on the Guru, even if you meditate just a tiny bit every day on the Guru, on the "Conscious Being dwelling in the Heart" (the Guru's form inside of your heart), He said, "I shall reveal to you the importance of those few seconds of meditation." Here He is not saying to meditate for a long time. No. He said, "Drop your mind into your heart and meditate on the Guru inside of your heart."

Verse 116

**Agocaraṁ tathā'gamyaṁ
nāma rūpa vivarjitam
Niḥśabdaṁ tadvijānīyāt
svabhāvaṁ brahma pārvati**

O Parvati! The Absolute is by nature impalpable, difficult to attain, beyond name, form and sound. You know this.

Here Lord Shiva is saying to Parvati, "To attain something that the mind can't perceive, can't name, can't understand, can't comprehend - so how do you think you will understand that?"

He said to Parvati, "You know how difficult it is? You are Yogamaya Yourself. You are the one who casts the Maya, so that You make it difficult for the people to find that, to understand that! But I shall reveal to You the deepness of that action of Yours! Why has the Supreme Lord made You who You are? I shall reveal to You why you have to do that."

Verse 117

Yathā gandhaḥ svabhāvena
karpūra kusumādiṣu
Śītoṣṇādi svabhāvena
tathābrahma ca śāśvatam

As fragrance is natural to flowers and camphor, cold and heat are natural phenomena. The Absolute is everlasting.

In all the flowers there is fragrance. Flowers and fragrance go hand in hand together, like fire and heat, like water and cold. So these are the "natural phenomena", but both go together. One can't exist without the other. Then it will not be fire! Water without coolness will not be water! Flower without fragrance will not be truly a flower, because even if you smell a flower and it seems not to have fragrance, yet in the deepness, in the essence, the fragrance is always there.

So here Bhagavan Shankar is saying that this connection between a Guru and a disciple is everlasting. There can't be a Guru without a disciple. There can't be a disciple without a Guru. So they go eternally together.

Verse 118

Svayaṁ tathāvidho bhūtvā
stātavayṁ yatra kutra cit
Kīṭa bhramara vattatra
dhyānaṁ bhavati tādṛśam

Attaining the condition of the Supreme, you may be anywhere. Just as a caterpillar is transformed into a butterfly by constantly meditating on the latter, one should meditate on the Lord to become like Him.

If you attain the Supreme, "you may be anywhere. Just as a caterpillar is transformed into a butterfly by constantly meditating on the latter, one should meditate on the Lord to become like Him." When the caterpillar is inside the cocoon, its mind is always fixed on when he will go out. The mind doesn't move left, right, because the caterpillar is not aware of anything else.

Here He said that "one should meditate on the Lord," one should meditate on the Guru, constantly, so that one can become alike. It doesn't matter where you are, space, time, it doesn't matter, it doesn't make any difference. You can meditate on your Guru even being in the South Pole and you'll receive the blessing equally as if you are seated next to the Guru. Because even if the Guru is seated here in the outside, the Guru is seated in the deepness of one's heart. Lord Shiva said, "Meditate on the Guru. Meditate on the Supreme Lord in the form of the Master and let one become like Him."

And you will see that very often: one who is truly surrendered to the Guru, their qualities also change. They start to look like the Guru, they start to act like the Guru, they start to think like the Guru. Even the appearance sometimes changes - when you travel in India, you notice that the Guru and a disciple very often look alike. This is due to how much they are surrendered. This is due to how much one is meditating on one's Master. The more the meditation is on the Master, the more the Grace of the Master shall shine upon the disciple.

Verse 119

Gurudhyānaṁ tathā kṛtvā
svayaṁ brahmamayo bhavet
Piṇḍe pade tathā rūpe
mukto'sau nātra saṁṣaya

A disciple himself becomes divine by meditating on the Guru. There is no doubt that one whose Kundalini is awake, with his prana steady, is liberated.

In the former verse He said that one should meditate on the Lord to become like Him.

Bhagavan Shankar is saying that when the Kundalini awakens, one has the control of the mind, one has the control of the prana, the breathing. So, when one has the control over the breathing and the prana, one is considered to be liberated, one attains a level of liberation. But when one meditates on the Guru, one becomes fully Divine. Here He is not talking just about liberation, but He is talking about the Inner Divinity, which is higher than liberation itself.

Śrī Pārvatī uvāca:

Verse 120

Piṇḍaṁ kiṁ tu mahādeva
padaṁ kiṁ samudāhṛtam
Rūpātītaṁ ca rūpaṁ kim
etadākhyāhi śankara

Parvati said: O Great Lord, what is 'Pindam' and how do you define 'Padam'; what is 'Roopam' and 'Roopatitam'? Tell this to me, O Shankar!

Parvati is asking Lord Shiva to explain to Her what 'Pindam' is. 'Pindam' means the seat, but also has other different meanings. One of the meanings of Pindam is the seat; another meaning of it is Shakti, or it can also mean 'ancestral'.

Then She asked, "How do you refer 'Padam'?" 'Padam' means the Feet. So 'Pindam' and 'Padam' here together define the Guru Himself. In this context, 'Pindam' is defined as the flow of energy which is constantly flowing through the Feet of the Master. That's why when one bows down to the Master's Feet, one is touched with that energy.

In the story of Kabirdasji (commentary of verse 97) – what was it that touched him when he was lying down on the step? The Guru's paduka. The paduka means the shoe, the slipper which the Master was wearing. But if the slipper can bless the disciple, imagine the Feet of the Master?

What is 'Rūpam'? Here it says that 'Rūpam' means the form. What is this form? What mystery does this form hold? Because everybody sees only with the physical eyes, the outside, the gross matter of the Master only. But that's not the reality! The Master is not just what one sees on the outside. There must be something greater than that what the Master is hiding. So, Parvati said, "Reveal to me that 'Rūpam' also. And reveal to me the 'Rūpatitam'. Reveal to me what is behind that actual form. What secret does this form of the Master hold, in the form and beyond that form? Which form lies beyond the form of the Master? Who is He?" Here Parvati is saying, "O Shankar, tell this to me! O Devadi Dev, You are the Lord of demigods, You are the only one who can reveal that to me."

Śrī Mahādeva uvāca:

Verse 121

Piṇḍaṁ kuṇḍalinī śaktiḥ
padaṁ haṁsamudāhṛtam
Rūpaṁ bindu riti jñeyaṁ
rūpātītaṁ nirañjana

Shree Mahadev said:
'Pindam' is Kundalini Shakti, 'Padam' is said to be 'hamsa' (prana); know 'Rūpam' to be the Blue Pearl and 'Rūpatitam' (beyond the Blue Bindu) is to be pure Being.

Piṇḍaṁ kuṇḍalinī śaktiḥ, here Mahadeva said that 'Pindam' is Kundalini Shakti. All the Shakti is flowing constantly inside of the Guru. In the Guru, the Kundalini is fully awakened, it's not in a dormant state. The Guru always dwells in an awakened state.

'Hamsa' stands also for purity and for something that can't be grasped.

"Know *'Rūpaṁ'* to be the Blue Pearl," Nowadays there are many blue pearls, but the Blue Pearl is unique - I am talking about the real one, not the painted one nor the manufactured one. It is said that in millions of pearls, one may get one real Blue Pearl. So here Bhagavan Shankar is saying that the *'Rūpaṁ'*, the form of the Master is like the Blue Pearl, which is very rare. It's not always that the

Guru incarnates in this world. There are many gurus, shishya gurus, like I explained earlier (commentary of verse 23), but the Satguru is unique. Out of millions, the Satguru's 'Rūpaṁ' manifests. Because not everybody - the shishya guru can't take you from the mundane world to the spiritual world, only the Satguru can do that.

Here He said that 'rūpātītaṁ', which means "beyond the Blue Bindu." Bhagavan Himself is represented as the Cosmic OM and the Bindu itself. The dot in the Sri Chakra is the Supreme Reality. Bhagavan is explaining that this word 'rūpātītaṁ' is the seat of the Guru. It is the purest of all and it is blue in colour. Here He defined that this Bindu is not red, as it is explained in the Devi Mahatmya or in the Sri Vidya. Here Bhagavan Shankar has given another meaning of the Bindu saying that this Bindu is blue in colour, which means the colour of infinity and stands for eternity - the one who absorbs all and can't be changed. Everything what is pale can change! But the dark dot itself, it can't be changed. That's why Krishna is referred as Shyam Sundar, the dark-coloured one. Whereas in Sri Vidya, it tells you that the Bindu is red and red stands for Shakti only, it stands for Prakriti.

He said that the Guru is never out of the Supreme pure Being. Even if in the outside it appears limited to the Prakriti Tattva, yet the Guru is never absorbed into the outside world, He is always absorbed into the Divine Consciousness.

Verse 122

Piṇḍe muktā pade muktā
rūpe muktā varānane
Rūpātīte tu ye muktās te
muktā nātra saṁśayaḥ

O Beautiful One, there is no doubt that He whose Kundalini is awakened, whose prana is steady, who has seen the Blue Bindu and even beyond, is truly liberated.

Here Bhagavan Shankar is explaining that a Guru has all these qualities. The Guru's Kundalini is constantly awakened, but He has control over it, which many people don't have. Because very often people think that their Kundalini is awakened, but in reality it's not. They go into the fantasy of the mind and that can be very dangerous. That's why Bhagavan Shankar here is referring to the one "whose prana is steady". Because when the Kundalini awakens - you see that very often in people who do Kundalini yoga, they are always in constant movement, no? *[Audience laughs]* But this is nothing to laugh about. It is a reaction. Because when the Kundalini is dormant and gets awakened, it's like a snake. The Kundalini is represented as a snake, no? And this energy vibrates, it's like a current inside the body, which shakes the body.

But Kundalini awakening doesn't mean only when you see somebody vibrating. No. Kundalini awakening means also when somebody has awakened into that state, but yet they have reached a certain level where the prana is stable; they have mastered the breathing, they have mastered the mind, so they are in a calm state – that's mastery! That's what we call breathless state, no? To enter samadhi. But to reach such a state of breathlessness, you have first to reach the state of mindlessness, because that Consciousness will not awake if the mind is active. Because the mind will always run according to how your breathing is. If somebody is breathing very harshly, the mind also runs in different ways, in many ways. But the ones, whose breathing is calm, they are mostly centred within their own Self. They are not extroverted, they are introverted.

Here Bhagavan Shankar carried on saying that it's not only the Kundalini being awakened and the control of the breathing. No. The focus also has to be steady. One has seen the blue light, the "Blue Bindu". One has one's mind focused into a single-pointed direction. They are not wandering around, but they are fixed and centred. This is very important – to reach that steadiness, to fix yourself. Only then one can go beyond that Bindu. So that's what is called liberation. When you reach above that, you are liberated. But all this happens only through the Grace of the Guru. Without the Grace of the Guru it's not possible!

Verse 123

**Svayaṁ sarvamayo bhūtvā
paraṁ tattvaṁ vilokayet
Parāt parataraṁ nānyat
sarva metannirālayam**

Experience the Highest Being by becoming everything yourself. There is nothing beyond THAT. All this (the world) is without basis.

"Experience the Highest Being by becoming everything yourself." Bhagavan Shankar is saying that when you meditate, it's not just to sit down and concentrate. To perceive the Supreme Reality you have to see everything inside of you. And you have to see you in everything, to break the barrier of difference. That's why I used to do the meditation where you see yourself in everything. Otherwise one is always in duality. One always sees, "I am here. You are there." But for the Guru, no. The Guru knows what is inside the heart of each person, because even if He is physically seated here, He is also seated inside the heart. So the Guru perceives Himself as an expansion of Himself in everything. So, "There is nothing beyond THAT. All this is without basis, the world is without basis," *sarva metannirālayam sarva metannirālayam*, which means that all is only the Supreme Reality. If you realise this connection, you realise that everything around you, everybody, the plants, the animals, the trees, the people, are eternally connected. There is a flow of energy that creates the balance of this world. That's why when sometimes something breaks through to that Higher Cosmos, there is a disbalance happening. Probably the disbalance will not happen here, it will happen somewhere else. But that disbalance is due to that 'break'. The one who is aware, they perceive the whole connection. They are inwardly interconnected

Verse 124

Tasyāvalokanaṁ prāpya
sarva saṅga vivarjitaḥ
Ekākī niḥspṛhaḥ śāntastiṣ
ṭhāset tatprasādataḥ

After experiencing the Godhead by the Guru's Grace, all your attachments and desires vanish. You become solitary tranquil and firmly stable (in the Self).

"After experiencing the Godhead by the Guru's Grace," here Bhagavan Shankar said that you can't experience the Ultimate by yourself. Even if you try in a hardest way, it's impossible without the Grace. But with the Grace of the Guru, everything which is impossible becomes possible. Here He said that even the Supreme Narayana Himself will manifest and reveal Himself only when there is the Grace of the Master.

Sarva saṅga vivarjitaḥ, "...your attachments and desires vanish," Once one has experienced the Supreme Reality, one sees the world completely different. One perceives the world in a different state. When one realises oneself, one's way of seeing, this world transforms itself, it changes!

"You become solitary tranquil and firmly stable (in the Self)." Here 'solitary' doesn't mean that when one reaches this state, one runs away into a cave. No. But one becomes more centred within oneself. One becomes more introverted, less extroverted. One enters the inner calmness, the inner peace and one's mind is fixed. The mind is not wandering around, it's not jumping around like the thought of an indecisive person who sometimes says 'yes', then says 'no' - 'yes', 'no' - 'yes', 'no' - 'no', 'yes'; then the person itself is confused and confuses everybody else. He said, "No." When one has attained the Grace of the Guru, and through the Grace of the Guru, one has attained the vision of the Lord and has experienced the Lord within one's own Self. One's mind becomes stable, it doesn't jump. There is no trace of doubt. There is no trace of judgement. There is no trace of unsureness inside.

Verse 125

Labdhaṁ vā'tha na labdhaṁ vā
svalpaṁ vā bahulaṁ tathā
Niṣkāmenaiva bhoktavyaṁ
sadā santuṣṭa cetasā

Whatever comes to you, be it little or much or even nothing – enjoy it with a contented mind and without attachment or desire.

Here Bhagavan Shankar is saying that one who is surrendered to the Feet of the Master should learn to accept whatever God gives. And if one accepts whatever God gives, one is not bothered, the mind is not worried, the mind is not disturbed. Even if they have little or much, or even if they don't have anything, they are content.

Here you see that normally people always expect something in return, no? You do something for someone and you expect that the person will say, "Thank you." or have some gratitude towards you. Paranthapa is saying, "I scratch your back, you scratch my back." I don't know. This is an African thing. *[Audience burst out laughing]* Scratching of the back?! *[Swamiji laughs]*

Lord Shiva says that if one is surrendered to the Feet of the Master, one is not bothered about what one gets and how much one gets; whether it is "...little or much or even nothing," one is content. You see that in the life of saints. They don't need much to be happy. Even if they don't have anything, they are still happy!

Verse 126

Sarvajña padam ityāhur
dehī sarvamayo budāḥ
Sadānandaḥ sadā śānto
ramate yatra kutra cit

After attaining the all-knowing state, an embodied soul becomes everything. Being always blissful and tranquil, such a one delights (in his own Self) wherever one may be.

"After attaining the all-knowing state, an embodied soul becomes everything." Bhagavan Shankar is saying that once by the Grace of the Master one attains the True Knowledge, *Brahma Jyaan* - it's not just a knowledge of the mind, but a knowledge of the Self - one attains Realisation, one perceives the same energy which is inside of oneself in everything. One becomes blissful and calm, tranquil. Why does one become tranquil? It is because one finds all within oneself. There is no need to look elsewhere for that happiness, because that happiness is seated inside of you. Because you yourself become this happiness! You yourself become Satchidananda. This is your True Self. You are Satchidananda.

You are this Eternal Bliss! So, He says that this - *ramate yatra kutra chit*, this may happen wherever you are; there is no time or space; but all is due to the Grace of the Master.

Verse 127

Yatraiva tiṣṭhate so'pi
sa deśaḥ puṇya bhājanam
Muktasya lakṣaṇaṁ devi
tavāgre kathitaṁ mayā

Wherever He dwells, that very place becomes holy. O Goddess! Thus have I described to you the characteristics of a liberated one.

Wherever He dwells, wherever He stays, wherever He is, that very place becomes holy. He says, "Holiness is not outside! Holiness is where the Guru is!" And if the Guru's Feet are inside the heart of the bhakta, wherever that bhakta is, that place becomes holy because there is no difference between the bhakta and the Guru.

"O Goddess! Thus have I described to you the characteristics of a liberated one." Here Bhagavan Shankar is saying that, "I described to you..." These are few qualities which a liberated soul possesses. Wherever He is, whatever He touches, everything becomes holy: the place, the things He uses, everything becomes sanctified with His energy and those things themselves emanate the Grace of the Master.

Verse 128

Upadeśas tathā devi
gurumārgeṇa muktidaḥ
Guru bhaktis tathā dhyānaṁ
sakalaṁ tava kīrtitam

O Goddess! I have explained the message to you: by following the path shown by the Guru, by devotion to the Guru, and meditation on Him, one attains salvation.

"O Goddess! I have explained the message to you," Here Bhagavan Shankar is saying that, even if Maha Devi, Maha Shakti is the personification of Knowledge Herself, yet Shiva, who is the Eternal Consciousness, is revealing the greatness of the Guru to Her.

"By following the path shown by the Guru, by devotion

to the Guru, and meditation on Him, one attains salvation." Here Bhagavan Shankar says, "All this that I have explained to you - one may attain it very easily just by having devotion to one's Guru. If one meditates on Him, one will attain salvation!"

He says, "You don't need to do much! You just need to follow what the Master asks of you. You have to have full faith in the Master. You just need to meditate on the Master's Feet. And if you are sincere in your spiritual practices, you'll attain salvation, you'll attain liberation!"

Verse 129

Anena yad bhavet kāryaṁ
tad vadāmi mahāmate
Lokopakārakaṁ devi
laukikaṁ tu na bhāvayet

O Wise One! I shall now speak to you of the work, which can be accomplished (by studying and reciting the Guru Gita). O Goddess! The powers accruing from this should be used only for the welfare of people and not for selfish gains.

"O Wise One!" Here Bhagavan Shankar stopped addressing Devi as "O Beautiful One!" But He also knows that Maha Devi is the "Wise One!" "I shall now speak to you of the work, which can be accomplished (by studying and reciting the *Guru Gita*)." Here Bhagavan Shankar is revealing the secret of the *Guru Gita*. What does this do for oneself? What is the effect of reading the *Guru Gita* every day with deep concentration, faith and devotion?

"O Goddess! The powers accruing from this should be used only for the welfare of people and not for selfish gains." Here Bhagavan Shankar is saying that whatever you receive through the Grace of the Master, even the punya that you receive by studying the *Guru Gita* is not for your own personal gain. You attain liberation, you attain a certain level of spirituality due to the Grace of the Master, and whatever is given by the Grace of the Master is not personally for you. Even if the Master has liberated you, it is always for the welfare of the humanity. Service to the people. Very often people think, "Oh, you know, I have attained that level. I have a certain realisation, that's it!" No. True Realisation makes you humble. And out of humbleness, you always help other people.

Here Bhagavan Shankar is saying to Parvati, "O Goddess! The powers which one has acquired through the service to the Guru, one should also use them for the welfare of people." This means that once you have attained liberation, once you have attained the Lotus

Feet of the Lord, once you have attained the Grace to be at the Master's Feet, you should always try to help others to be also on that path of surrender. Help others to free themselves, to liberate themselves!

In the *Gita*, chapter 18, in the last verses, Bhagavan Krishna Himself also said, "What I have given you, what I have said to you, O Arjuna, this is for humanity." He says that a bhakta's life is always to help others to be free. If somebody is drowning himself into illusion, help them to go out of that illusion. Free them! So that as you are liberated you shall also liberate others.

Verse 130

Laukikāt karmaṇo yānti
jñāna hīna bhavāṇavam
Jñāni tu bhāvayet sarvaṁ
karma niṣkarma yat kṛtam

The ignorant, by using the Guru Gita for selfish ends, swirl in the ocean of worldliness. The actions of the Enlightened become means for their liberation. Such people need not suffer or experience the fruit of their deeds.

"The ignorant, by using the *Guru Gita* for selfish ends,

swirl in the ocean of worldliness." Here Bhagavan Shankar is saying that if you have received the *Guru Gita*, you have received the Grace of the Master, you have received the Guru Mantra, yet you are still ignorant and utilise what God has given you for selfish aims, then you will never be free. They will be drowned in the worldliness, which means that Maya will pull them and cover them, blind them.

"The actions of the Enlightened become means for their liberation. Such people need not suffer or experience the fruit of their deeds." Here Bhagavan Shankar is saying that those who utilise the *Guru Gita* and attain Enlightenment by concentrating - the *Guru Gita* here stands for the knowledge of surrendering to the Master's Feet - who listen to what it is said in the Guru Gita and practises it - they become liberated. So He says that whoever is surrendered by following what is written in the *Guru Gita*, they attract liberation to them, through the Guru's Grace. Just by surrendering to the Feet of the Master one breaks the karmic consequences of all the past sins, the past karmas of many lives, which have to be expiated. So the Guru becomes like an eraser which wipes clean the past karmas. And the one who is truly surrendered doesn't need to experience any past karmas.

Verse 131

Idaṁ tu bhaktibhāvena
paṭhate śṛṇute yadi
Likhitvā tat pradātavyaṁ
tat sarvaṁ saphalaṁ bhavet

Reading or hearing the Guru Gita with devotion, or making a copy of it and giving it to another, would earn great merit.

Here Bhagavan Shankar is saying that If you read, or even if you don't know how to read, if you just listen about the greatness of the Guru with an opened heart full of devotion, it will bring good punya to you. It will increase your bank account balance in heaven. But if you just listen to it and read it as a novel, it will not help, it will not bear any punya.

He also says that if you just make a copy of the *Guru Gita*, or buy a copy from the shop *[Swamiji is referring to the Bhakti Marga Shop and audience laughs]*, and give it to someone, it will also bring good merit. So by giving it, talking about it to somebody else, by saving someone else, He said that it will bring good punya to yourself.

Verse 132

Gurugītātmakam devi
śuddha tattvaṁ mayoditam
Bhava vyādhi vināśārthaṁ
svayameva japetsad

O Goddess! I have revealed to you the pure truth contained in the Guru Gita. To overcome the malady of worldliness you should always repeat it.

"O Goddess! I have revealed to you the pure truth contained in the *Guru Gita*." Here Bhagavan Shankar has revealed in the most simple way how important is to serve one's Master.

To overcome the delusion or the sickness of the worldliness, one should always read and repeat the *Guru Gita* constantly. He said that if you want to free your mind, if you want to have a peace of mind, read the *Guru Gita*. Meditate on the Guru. Chant the Guru's Name. Meditate on His form.

Verse 133

**Gurugāitākṣaraikaṁ tu
mantra rājamimaṁ japet
Anye ca vividhā mantrāḥ
kalāṁ nārhanti ṣoaśīm**

Each letter of the Guru Gita is a supreme mantra. Repeat it. All other mantras of diverse kinds do not have even one-sixteenth of its power.

"Each letter of the *Guru Gita* is a supreme mantra. Repeat it." Chant it daily. "All other mantras of diverse kinds do not have even one-sixteenth of its power." Here Bhagavan Shankar is saying that just by chanting the Name of the Guru, by concentrating on the Guru, it covers all the other mantras. It's only by the Guru's Grace that all the other mantras receive their power, so why not chant the name of the Master?

Śrī Mahādeva uvāca:

Verse 134

Ananta phalamāpnoti
guru gītā japena tu
Sarva pāpa praśamanaṁ
sarva dāridrya nāśanam

By repeating the Guru Gita, endless rewards are obtained, all sins are destroyed, and all privations are put to an end.

"By repeating the *Guru Gita,*" by chanting the Glory of the Guru, by constant remembrance of the Guru, "endless rewards are obtained, all sins are destroyed, and all privations are put to an end." Here Bhagavan Shankar is saying that only by reading, chanting and meditating on the Guru; by chanting the glory of the Guru, as it is described in the *Guru Gita*, one obtains endless merits. So everything that one desires is fulfilled. All the sins are put to an end. So just by surrendering to the Feet of the Master and by meditating on the Master, one will automatically receive all that one really needs in one's life.

Verse 135

**Kāla mṛtyu bhayaharaṁ
sarva saṅkaṭa nāśanam
Yakṣa rākṣasabhūtānāṁ
coravyāghrabhayāpaham**

The Guru Gita delivers one from the fear of death, and the fear of yakshas, rakshasas, ghosts, thieves and wild animals. It stalls all mishaps and misfortunes.

"The *Guru Gita*," the Glories of the Guru, "delivers one from the fear of death." The Guru frees one from the cycle of birth and death and makes one realise that one is as eternal as the Atma. Whoever chants the *Guru Gita*, whoever trusts the Guru truly, whoever chants the name of the Guru with devotion and meditates on the form of the Guru should not fear anything, should not even fear the demons, the ghosts, thieves, wild animals, nothing! The Guru removes all the misfortunes and misunderstandings.

Verse 136

Mahā vyādhi haraṁ sarvaṁ
vibhūti siddhidaṁ bhavet
Athavā mohanaṁ vaśyaṁ
svayameva japet sadā

It drives away all diseases and confers wealth and siddhis, extraordinary accomplishments, such as the power of enchanting others. Repeat it always.

The Guru's Name "drives away all diseases and confers wealth and siddhis". The Guru gives spiritual wealth and also all things which one needs in the material world. And the one who is truly surrendered attains all kind of "siddhis, extraordinary accomplishments, such as the power of enchanting others. Repeat it always." Here Bhagavan Shankar is saying that the ones who chant the Guru's Name acquire *Vashikaran*, they will become Vashikaran themselves. Because they start to shine another light, not their own; they start to shine the Divine Light and that Light attracts. As the moth is attracted from far away by the light and comes to the light, in the same way, the ones who are surrendered to the Master, who have the Grace of the Master with them, they become an enchanter for others. So, they attract the people, bring them on the right way. They start to reflect the Light of the Guru. Then there is no difference between the bhakta and the Guru, because the Guru shines His Light upon the bhakta.

Verse 137

**Vastrāsane ca dāridryaṁ
pāṣāṇe rogasambhavaḥ
Medinyāṃ duḥkhamāpnoti
kāṣṭhe bhavati niṣphalam**

Repeating the Guru Gita while sitting on a cloth seat one gets poverty; on a stone seat diseases arise; on the ground one gets sorrow; on a wooden seat the japa would be fruitless.

Bhagavan Shankar is saying that by chanting the *Guru Gita* seated on a cloth, one will become poor. Here poverty doesn't mean poverty of the outside, but He said by chanting the *Guru Gita* one will be freed from attachments.

And if one is seated on a stone, one will get rid of the diseases which the mind always creates. And one who is seated on the ground will get rid of sorrow. And the one who is seated on a wooden seat, the japa will become fruitless. Here I would say that it will bear its fruits; not the punya of the outside, but the inner punya. Bhagavan Shankar is not talking about the outside reality, He's talking about the inner reality.

So, He said that one should not chant merely thinking on what one is seated, on what the mind is seated. Very often, when people are doing their sadhana, they always think on what they are sitting, believing that according to the seat they will get certain punya, no? Here Bhagavan Shankar is saying, "No. You should not bother about the seat. Your focus should not be on what your behind is sitting on. Your focus should be on the Guru inside of your heart. Then you will have all the punya! But if your focus is diverted to the outside, then it will not bear any fruit." Here Bhagavan Shankar is saying that this reading of the *Guru Gita* doesn't need to be done on a particular place.

There is no direction to turn to while reading the *Guru Gita*. There is no special seat to be used. What will benefit you is only the devotion that you have in your heart. That's the only thing you need while reading the *Guru Gita*. Whenever you read the *Guru Gita*, chant the Guru's name, sing the praises of the Guru, you must be focused only in your heart. The reading of the *Guru Gita* is not bound by any external matters. Because what is in the external will always bring external things.

Verse 138

Kṛṣṇājine jñanasiddhir
mokṣaśrī vyāghracarmaṇi
Kuśāsane jñānasiddhiḥ
sarvasiddhistu kambale

Repeating it (while sitting) on the skin of a black deer, one attains knowledge; on a tiger skin, one gets the wealth of liberation; on a Kush, reed or rush seat, one attains knowledge; on a woollen blanket, gets all attainments.

But if you really want to focus on the traditional way of sitting and if you truly want to achieve higher perfection, repeat the *Guru Gita* "sitting on the skin of a black deer". So if you sit on the skin of a black deer, you get knowledge. *[Someone in the audience asks something and Swamiji answers, "No, we don't have it in the shop!" Audience burst out laughing. Swamiji says referring to his seat, "We have it here! We'll send them to Paranthapa, he will start a business soon."]* Here Bhagavan Shankar is saying that if you want to attain knowledge, then you should sit "on the skin of a black deer".

If you want to attain the "wealth of liberation", you should sit "on a tiger skin", but you have to kill the tiger with your own hands first *[Audience burst out laughing]*, or if you are lucky, you find one which died by itself. No, I am just joking! You see, this is the African way.

When I was in Kenya, they were saying that the Maasai, their men to get married have to fight with a lion with bare hands. Only then they can get married. *[Audience burst out laughing]* So, that's why in certain cultures you see that there are many women and there is only one man... *[Audience laughs heartily]*... the alpha, the rest is gone! *[Swamiji burst out laughing]* No, I am just joking right now, to wake you up, otherwise you are sleeping. Don't start killing, because killing of any kind is completely wrong.

So, Bhagavan Shankar is saying that to get punya, "wealth of liberation", one should sit on a skin of a tiger. Of course, the tiger must not be killed, but should die naturally. But these are only punyas, you know? Specific aims.

What is the aim of a bhakta? If the bhakta aims only for knowledge, then it's this kind of meditation, this kind of japa. If the bhakta is aiming for wealth of liberation, then sitting on a tiger's skin will help them. But if one aims for Brahma Jyaan, True Knowledge, here Bhagavan Shankar, Shiva said that one should sit on Kush grass - we have it in the shop. *[Audience burst out laughing]*

So, if you aim for True Knowledge of the Self, you should sit on Kush grass or on a seat made of reeds.

And if one wants to get all desires fulfilled, one should sit on a woollen blanket, which is easier. So this is for all accomplishments, all attainments. So you see, the Guru makes it easy. If you want to attain everything, just sit on a woollen mat. That will be enough, not that complicated.

You see, the aim of different people varies, no? Not everybody, even if they hear the *Guru Gita*, even if they hear the explanation, they agree with it. Some will say, "Oh, you know, it's just 'bla, bla, bla'. These are just stories," all this, you know? But these stories have deeper meaning behind them.

If you see the ingenious way of how Vyasa wrote the *Guru Gita* - he didn't write it only for one kind of people. He wrote it for many kinds of people. So each kind of people will understand it according to their level of understanding. If somebody dwells in a very low frequency, they will also understand it, because they will find part of themselves into it; so this will also react on them. That's how he brings the people to a higher degree of spirituality, from the lower, from wherever, however they are. He said, "Everybody is welcome! Liberation is for everybody! Not for one kind of people only, but for all, for all humanity!" That's why he gives different steps.

Verse 139

Kuśairvā dūrvayā devi
āsane śubhra kambale
Upaviśya tato devi
japedekāgra mānasaḥ

O Goddess! The Guru Gita should be repeated with single-minded devotion while sitting on a reed or rush seat covered with a white cloth.

Here Bhagavan Shiva, after given all the description of on what one should sit to attain what... *[Audience laughing]*... because the seat - why is He saying that? Why is He emphasising the seat in this part of the *Guru Gita*? The seat is very important. Your asan - even Krishna in the *Bhagavad Gita* spoke about the asan. The asan is not just to take a cushion and put it under you, and sit on it saying, "I am happy! I feel comfortable." No. The asan carries your vibration, your energy. That's why where you have your asan, nobody else should sit on your place.

Of course, not here, like I said during the *Gita* course, in a temple there is no fixed place for people to sit, apart from the priest and the Guru. The rest, for the bhakta, it's public space for everybody.

But at home, when you do your sadhana, it's very important to keep your asan. It's important that nobody else, even your wife, husband or somebody else, sit on your asan. Because your whole vibration is concentrated there. When you sit on your asan and meditate, the energy which is created during the time of your sadhana is ever-present. Even if you are not there physically, your asan always keeps that energy. That flow of energy is always present on it. And when you come back again and sit on it, you are reconnected with that energy again. That's why it is important to have your own asan, your own seat. That's why Bhagavan Shankar is emphasising here that the seat is very important! Imagine that somebody, who is very materialistic, sits on a tiger's skin and does his sadhana. And you, who are longing for devotion to the Lord, come and sit there. What will happen? Automatically you will baffle yourself from your aim of spirituality to the material aim. Because that's what you also take from that asan.

So, that's why it's very important to know – to keep your asan. That's why Shiva is talking about the importance of the seat here.

Kuśairvā dūrvayā devi āsane śubhra kambale "O Goddess! The *Guru Gita* should be repeated with single-minded devotion," and if you want to bear the full attainment, the true knowledge of the *Guru Gita*, the true understanding of the *Guru Gita*, you should sit on a Kush grass "covered with a white cloth."

So He said that you should take a Kush grass mat and cover it with a white cloth, and then you can sit on it.

But above all, the emphasis in this verse is the "single-minded devotion". Earlier I have said that if you read the *Guru Gita* just as a novel, it will not bear any fruit. It will just be, "What is this Swami talking about? What did this Vyasa write? What is this Shiva talking about?" But if you read it with a "single-minded devotion", if you read it with devotion, and your mind is focused on the Feet of the Master, only then you will bear the fruit of what you are doing.

Verse 140

Dhyeyaṁ śuklaṁ ca śāntyarthaṁ
vaśye raktāsanaṁ priye
Abhicāre kṛṣṇavarṇaṁ
pītavarṇaṁ dhanāgame

O Beloved! A white seat is suitable for obtaining peace, a red one for the power of charming others, a black one for exorcising evil spirits and a yellow one for acquiring wealth.

Here Bhagavan Shiva is saying to Parvati, "O Beloved! I shall tell you now the effect of colour on the sadhak.

Because it's not just the seat but the colour that you wear, your clothes also vibrate and react on you. Imagine that somebody is wearing a very terrible green colour. I am sure everybody will notice it, even if they don't say it. They would look at it thinking, "Eww!" So you know that colour does make an impression on people.

Here Bhagavan Shankar is saying, "O Beloved! A white seat is suitable for obtaining peace," That's why when you do your sadhana, it's very important to dress in white, because it is calm. It's not aggressive.

"A red one for the power of charming others," so the red colour - imagine that a mataji comes with a deep red lipstick - everybody will turn around and look. And they will say, "Have you seen her lipstick?" It's true! That means that colour reacts. So the red here, He said is for the power of charming. You know that very well, red rose - what does it stand for? It is said that if you give a white rose, it is for friendship, but if you give a red rose, it means more than friendship, so it's a charming red. That's why for Valentine's day all the roses everywhere are red.

"A black one for exorcising evil spirits." Very often people in the mind perceive black as something negative, no? Here Bhagavan Shankar said, "No." Black is Kalaratri. Yesterday, Ma Bhagavati was dressed in black, no? *[Swamiji is referring to the Navaratri Celebrations 2014]*

Krishna is black! Bhagavan Krishna and Kalaratri Devi are black. Yesterday you saw how wonderful She was, all-terrifying. But for the one with an open heart, She is the loving Mother! There is nothing to fear. But if you have evil qualities inside of you - for that quality, She will appear very ferocious and terrifying. That's why people very often get scared when they see Her. But that instant reaction of seeing Kalaratri in that way, by recognising the dark outside means that there is something dark inside. But if there is light inside, one will recognise only the light outside.

So Bhagavan Shankar here is saying that the black colour, if put on a seat of Kush grass mat, on a Kush seat, it helps to exorcise evil spirits. By meditating, chanting the *Guru Gita* seated on a black cloth, it pushes away all negative spirits.

And on a yellow cloth one acquires wealth. Here Bhagavan Shankar is again talking for different kind of people saying that if one's mind aims to attain material gain, then, He said that you should do your sadhana, you should chant the *Guru Gita* seated on a yellow cloth. But under the cloth there should always be the Kush grass mat.

Verse 141

**Uttare śānti kāmastu
vaśye pūrvamukho japet
Dakṣiṇe māraṇaṁ proktaṁ
paścime ca dhanāgama**

Repeating the Guru Gita facing north would enable you to obtain peace; facing east would enable you to captivate others; facing south would enable you to kill (an enemy); facing west would enable you to acquire wealth.

In the previous verse, we have seen how colour affects one while meditating on the *Guru Gita* and which quality one acquires. Here Bhagavan Shankar carried on explaining to Goddess Parvati how important is the impact of a specific direction on those who meditate on the *Guru Gita*.

"Repeating the *Guru Gita* facing north would enable you to obtain peace." So facing north while chanting the *Guru Gita*, the Glory of the Guru, one will attain a peaceful life.

Facing east would enable you to captivate others, so by meditating and chanting the *Guru Gita* seated towards the east one becomes radiant, and this will make a certain impact upon other people. The Light will shine. The Guru's Light will shine through the bhakta and automatically people are attracted to that shininess.

Because a spiritual person carries a certain glow, which makes that person different when compared to other people. Whenever people meet a spiritual person, especially in the outside world, they automatically think, "That person is a bit strange." It's strange to the mind, because at that moment they perceive a certain glow in that person and they will interpret it according to their own level of understanding. Due to the outside world they perceive the Divine glow as something strange. However, this glow which one radiates is the Guru Himself, the Light of the Guru shining upon the devotee, and that Light captivates. Here this word *pūrvamukho japet* means that it doesn't only glow, but automatically people can see it. It's a convincing glow, which radiates through the devotee, the bhakta. It's not just a normal glow, but it's special, because it reacts on the people.

Facing south would enable you to kill a specific enemy - but know only thing, your greatest enemy is not outside of you, your greatest enemy is inside of you. It is *ahankara*, your pride, your ego. That's the great enemy! So here Lord Shiva is saying that by chanting the *Guru Gita*, by meditating on the *Guru Gita* facing south will sort your enemy out. But sometimes the outside enemy is also important. Because if you have an enemy in the outside, it will always disturb you, no? So it's good that you get rid of it from your mind, so that you don't concentrate on it, so that you are free from it.

Facing west would enable you to acquire spiritual and material wealth. Here Bhagavan Shankar is revealing that the Guru is giving both, the spiritual wealth and the material wealth.

Therefore, by chanting the *Guru Gita* while facing these four direction, one acquires specific blessings.

Actually, this is also a test from Lord Shiva. If you look at the pattern of all these instructions: meditating on a specific seat, meditating facing a certain direction - you will see that by saying that, Lord Shiva is clearly defining the aim of an individual. The one who aims for spiritual advancement doesn't fall into that category. Because the one who is dear to the Guru doesn't long for this. Then, they are focused on the One who is seated in the Sahasrara, the Bindu, the Blue Pearl, as I explained earlier (commentary of verse 121). And that is not bound by any direction, it's beyond all directions. It's seated above the bhakta, constantly! So by that, you see clearly what is the aim of the bhaktas, what they really want. Because a true bhakta doesn't bother about these things. But the ones who are only focused on dogmatism and narrow-mindedness, "It has to be like this... like this... like this," they fall into this category, which Lord Shiva has just explained.

There is a wonderful story that shows how the Guru tests the bhaktas through these qualities, by seeing their true nature.

A long time ago, there was a Rishi by the name of Vedasagara, which means the ocean of the *Vedas*. He was a master of the shastras, the *Vedas*, the *Puranas* and of course his ashram, which was situated by the Kaveri river. It was very well-known. He used to sit in this wonderful serene place by the Kaveri river teaching the shastras to his disciples. He used to impart this knowledge to his bhaktas, but he was very careful because he knew that True Knowledge can't be handled by everybody and should be given only to the true devotee. Why should you give something to somebody who can't handle it or who doesn't deserve it? For sure they will go elsewhere and sell it away. So he was very cautious of accepting his disciples; first he would examine them.

One day two students, two shishyas came to him. Their names were Ramasharma and Krishnasharma. For sure they were brothers. They came to Vedasagara and asked him if he would accept them as his students. Vedasagara told them, "Fine! But before I answer you this question, I would like you to stay in the ashram until you finish the exam."

Because to learn you have to take exams, no? It's like when you go to a certain well-known university. Before you are accepted, you are always put through tests. And you are accepted only if you pass the tests. Because that means that you have a certain potential of glorifying that university. Otherwise, what will be the use of just taking anybody who would bring shame to that university? Imagine you try to enter Harvard University without passing the tests – they will never accept you! Imagine you will always fail your exams and then you will say, "I went to Harvard, but look, I failed my exams. That's my certificate!" What would they do with that? It would be a shame. The people would say, "This Harvard University is very shameful!" That's why they test the students in order to get the best ones. Because they take the best ones from the world. Then they say about the other ones, "Another school will handle them." So like that, Vedasagara said to them, "Stay in the ashram and wait. Accept the exam and then we will see afterwards."

As the first lesson he taught them the mantra: *Gurur brahmā gurur viṣṇur gururdevo maheśvaraḥ Guru sākshāt parabrahma tasmai śrī gurave namaḥ* (this is the mantra that we chant during the Guru Puja). He explained to them in deep detail about this: the Guru is the Creator, the Guru is the protector and the Guru is the destroyer. And the Guru is above the Trimurti as *sākshāt parabrahma*. Then, he asked them, "Do you understand?" And they said, "Yes sir, we understand."

One day, it was Ekadasi – you see this is the fasting once a month, or sometimes twice a month, which is a must to do. Especially if you are a Vaishnava, it is very important to fast at least on Ekadasi. Because the Lord Himself is well pleased with the one who fasts on Ekadasi.

So it was Ekadasi and Vedasagara woke his disciples up very early in the morning. He told them, "Today is Ekadasi and this Ekadasi is very dear to both Mahavishnu and Lord Shiva." And on that day people should fast strictly and not eat anything - because each Ekadasi is different. In some Ekadasi days you are allowed to eat certain things, but in other Ekadasi days you are not allowed to eat at all. So, on that Ekadasi it was very important not to eat anything. Furthermore, Vedasagara told them that on that day it was very important to go around the secret hill, to do *parikrama*. So he instructed them, "Go around the hill and come back before sunset!" Both of them answered, "Yes!"

The sacred hill was not near, it was very far away. They walked until they finally reached Devalayam, the place of pilgrimage. They went around the temple and they were very exhausted. Because in India is very hot, and in that heat, they were not allowed even to drink a little bit of water, nothing! They were sweating, they were thirsty and they were tired. And as you know, when you are in that state, you also start to become grumpy. After the parikrama, they went into the temple and met the *pujari*. The pujari offered them *Prasad* from the temple and offered them *theertham*, which means water to drink. At that moment, Ramasharma remembered what the Guru had ordered them. The Guru had said, "This day is very important and you should not eat anything! You should keep complete fast and you should come back before sunset!" So he was a bit hesitant to accept the Prasad and to accept the theertham also. When the priest of the temple saw that both Ramasharma and Krishnasharma were a bit hesitant, he said, "I see that you are a bit hesitant, but this time is very difficult! So, you don't need to follow the order of your Guru. How would your Guru know that you have not obeyed him? He is so far away. Take it! Eat It!"

Krishnasharma was so hungry - his stomach was speaking all kinds of languages... *[Audience burst out laughing]* that he could not bear it anymore. As the priest said, "How would the Guru know about it?" So, he just happily drank the water and ate the food. However, Ramasharma chose to stick to what the Guru had ordered. He took it in his hand and said, "When the Guru gives the permission, then I shall eat." They returned back to the ashram and, of course, the Guru knew about this incident, but didn't say anything. He carried on like normal as if he didn't know anything.

One day the Guru was teaching them some lesson, and all of a sudden they noticed a fire spreading all around the ashram. They were completely surrounded by the fire and the only way out was - because you see, an ashram normally is built near a river. Like I said earlier, this ashram of Vedasagara was located by the Kaveri river... Kaveri is in Andhra (Ah! I remember once I was by the Kaveri river... Yeah! There are crocodiles in that river. Once we were standing there on the river - you know, I was young at that time, I am a bit old - so there were stones, I was jumping on the stones and then a man said, "Oh, be careful! This is a crocodile!" Do you remember, mum? You don't remember? Ah, you are too old already! So that's okay. He said, "Don't jump on this one! It's a crocodile!" *[Swamiji laughs]* It looked like a stone. I didn't jump. Maybe I should have...)

The only way out of this fire was by a small boat, but only two people could enter into the boat and save their lives. So Vedasagara immediately said to his disciples, "You both go into the boat and save yourselves! As you have taken my shelter, my *kartavya*, my duty is to look after you. So let me burn. Anyways, I am old. Who will care? At least you are still young. It would be sad to lose your life at such a young age." When Krishnasharma had heard that, he rushed quickly into the boat. As the Guru said that, immediately like a flash, he was already in the boat, seated, waiting for Ramasharma. At that moment, Ramasharma bowed down to the Guru and said, "Gurudev, please forgive me! I can't follow your advice right now. You have told us that the ultimate goal of a devotee, of a bhakta, is to serve the Guru and always protect the Guru. No matter what happens, the bhakta should always protect the Guru. This is our dharma! The greatest dharma of the bhakta is to always serve and protect the Guru. I can't go! You go! Anyway, what would the society lose if I die? I have not brought anything to the society, whereas you are a respected saint. And if you die, the society will lose someone far more important. Please take the boat, Gurudev!" So saying that Ramasharma forced the Guru into the boat. As the Guru touched the boat, the whole fire disappeared.

All this was an illusion created by Vedasagara himself to test his two students. He wanted to test their devotion. He wanted to see how much they were devoted to him. Then he said, "The pujari in the temple on the Ekadasi day was myself." Thus he revealed to them that in that occasion he was already testing them. Ramasharma was qualified to stay in the ashram, whereas Krishnasharma was sent back home. Vedasagara said, "Ramasharma is the only one who is qualified to surrender to the Guru." And of course, such bhaktas receive the Grace of Guru-bhakti not only from the Guru, but from the Ultimate Himself.

Verse 142

Mohanaṁ sarva bhūtānāṁ
bandhamokṣakaraṁ bhavet
Deva rāja priyakaraṁ
sarva loka vaśaṁ bhavet

By reciting the Guru Gita, acquiring the power to enchant all creatures and all the worlds, one becomes a darling of gods and rulers and gets liberation from all bondages.

Here Lord Shiva is saying that those who recite the *Guru Gita* daily, they don't affect only the people and the surroundings, but they also affect the lower species of nature, which means that the animals which are around also benefit from the blessing of the *Guru Gita*. Furthermore, all the three words, which means Patal Loka, Bhu Loka and Swarga Loka, the three, hell, earth and heaven are also blessed by those who recite the *Guru Gita*.

One becomes dear to the gods, because when the blessing of the Guru is present, automatically the gods, the devas are there. And finally those who chant the *Guru Gita* daily, they achieve liberation at the end of life, they are freed from all karmic bondages. Such is the Grace of the Master. Such is the Love of the Master.

Verse 143

Sarveṣāṁ stambhanakaraṁ
guṇānāṁ ca vivardhanam
Duṣkarma nāśanaṁ caiva
sukarma siddhidaṁ bhavet

The Guru Gita grants the power of paralysing hostile creatures, nurtures and nourishes good qualities, neutralises bad actions and brings deeds to fulfilment.

"The *Guru Gita* grants the power of paralysing hostile creatures," Let's say you are being attacked. Just by mere concentration on the Guru, the Guru transfers the energy from Him to the person and/or to the creatures. Automatically they are paralysed. But here 'paralysed' doesn't mean that somebody will get paralysed, but it is the power inside of them. Their motive is the one which will get paralysed. Let's say, for example, a lion is about to attack you. Just by closing your eyes and thinking of the Guru, the motive of the lion will change automatically inside itself and it will go away.

There is a story similar to that... *[Swamiji asks someone in the audience, "Pepe, do you remember?" Someone in the audience said something and Swamiji answered, "But, I can't remember it. So I am asking Pritala if he could look into his file, because, you see, he always has a file inside of him. So until he looks for it... are you still looking? It's a famous saint actually. Ah, he remembers a joke. Tell the joke! No, don't tell me! Tell it to the people.]*

Pritala: A missionary was in the jungle and suddenly a lion came. And the missionary prayed, "Oh God, please let the lion have a Christian thought!" The lion said, "Lord, bless this food." *[Swamiji and audience burst out laughing]*

SV: So, that was... my story is not coming, but it was nice! *[Audience laughs heartily]* Ah! He remembered! He is showing me a face of remembrance *[Audience laughs heartily]* Come! Come! Here the reappearance of Pritala! *[Audience laughing and clapping]*

Pritala: It was Saint Nicholas. You know, one time Saint Nicholas, at this time, they didn't like the Christian people, so they were transferred to the 'dessert' *[Swamiji corrects Pritala saying, "desert". Swamiji and audience burst out laughing. Swamiji, while laughing, says, "So they were transformed into dessert for the lion." Swamiji and audience laugh heartily. Swamiji finally says, "So, he already forgot" Swamiji and audience burst out laughing again]*

Pritala: "Okay, forget it! It's something else, it's something like this... *[Swamiji says while laughing, "We forgot!"]*... Saint Nicholas was dead long time ago, but everybody knew, especially the prisoners, knew that Saint Nicholas was their best friend. Because when people were in prison and prayed to Saint Nicholas, they were freed and miraculously transported to their home. You know, in the church of Saint Nicholas in France, in Saint-Nicolas-de-Port, the church was full of the chains of the prisoners. It was so full that in the year 1600 the priest who was taking care of the church wanted to get rid of all these chains, and he filled 10 chariots full of the chains of the prisoners who were hanging their chains in the church as they were being freed by Saint Nicholas's Grace.

Once a man was taken by the Muslims. When the executioner was standing before him with his big sword ready to cut his head, he prayed, "Please Saint Nicholas help me!" At that moment the sword was hanging in the air and the executioner could not bring it down. Everybody was shocked and the superior of the executioner said, "Let him go!"

[Swamiji says, "Okay. At least he remembered something. I am still not remembering. So, that's fine. It doesn't matter.] Actually, this was a wonderful story how Saint Nicholas subdued the hand of the executioner. This is due to the faith they had. He mentioned that many chains were broken. Even now when you go there, you see some of the chains are still there.

The one who is concentrated on the Master, "nurtures and nourishes good qualities," the one who is surrendered to the Guru is automatically transformed;

the good qualities become stronger and stronger, neutralising all the bad ones inside of oneself. And all the deeds become purified and sanctified.

Verse 144

Asiddhaṁ sādhayet kāryaṁ
navagraha bhayāpaham
Duḥsvapna nāśanaṁ caiva
susvapna phala dāyakam

It accomplishes impossible tasks, delivers one from the fear of harm from the nine planets, puts an end to bad dreams, and yields the fruit of all good dreams.

The *Guru Gita* "accomplishes impossible tasks." For the one who trusts in the Guru, whatever is impossible for the mind becomes possible.

"Delivers one from the fear of harm from the nine planets." You know very well that the planets have an effect on people. But, whoever is surrendered to the Guru should not fear the effect of the planets, because the Guru protects him.

There are three planets, Rahu, Ketu and Shani (Saturn), which always create disbalance. So whenever they are in a certain constellation, they can bring seven years of pain into the life of somebody. That's what is said, no? You are going through Shani Kaal or Rahu Kaal or Ketu Kaal. And then the priest will tell you, "Do this prayer." or "Do that prayer." and then you appease the influence of the planets. What is happening during that prayer time? You are rotating, you are changing the access through the mantras, through your belief.

So, He said that if one chants the *Guru Gita* every day, for the one who meditates on the Guru every day, the effect of the planets become favourable; it stops the negative effect of the planets.

It "puts an end to bad dreams, and yields the fruit of all good dreams." By stopping the effect of the planets – as you know, the planets do affect the people. When the Moon is full, inside of your body itself, your body goes through lots of changes and especially in the mind – the mind, the mental level is very active during that time. That's why it is said that during full Moon, you should not eat too much, because the water level in your body increases. Like the sea, during full Moon, the water of the sea always reaches high tide. In the body also, during full Moon time, even if you eat little, you already feel full. So it does make an effect on your body, because your body is made of water. How many percent? Sixty-five percent. Sixty-five percent of the body is made up of water. So, as the full Moon reacts on the water element, it automatically also reacts on the body. And if it reacts on the body, it reacts on the mind. So, that's why on full Moon days, we say, "Do OM Healing!" OM Healing is very good during a full Moon. What is happening during OM Healing at that moment? You are imprinting the cosmic sound, you are making each cell of your body vibrate this cosmic sound. So automatically, in place of going crazy, you feel good! You feel calm, you are in a meditative mood. Therefore it brings positiveness to you.

So He says, "If you read the *Guru Gita* and meditate on the Guru every day, these planets will not affect you!" You will always be protected, whether it is full Moon or not! Whether Saturn is passing through your constellation or not. It will not bother you because you are protected. The Guru shields the disciple.

Verse 145

Sarva śānti karaṁ nityaṁ
tathā vandhyā suputradam
Avaidhavya karaṁ strīṇāṁ
saubhāgya dāyakaṁ sadā

It always bestows peace in every situation, grants a son to a barren woman, maintains the happiness of a married woman by ensuring that she does not become a widow, and brings good fortune.

"It always bestows peace in every situation." It "grants a son" to the people who don't have a son, to "a barren woman." It "maintains the happiness" in the family and makes sure that a woman "does not become a widow," which means, it will make the woman die first, *[Audience burst out laughing]* and that brings good fortune to the family.

You see in the Hindu tradition, probably not now, but at the time when Vyasa wrote this, 5000 years ago, it was considered a curse if the husband died before the wife. But nowadays it doesn't matter. It changed. Nowadays, divorce has sorted these things out. So, it was considered a blessing if the wife died first. Do you know why? There is a secret behind that. Because if the husband died first, the family of the husband would be very cruel to the woman. And they will always blame the woman. Especially if the mother-in-law was still alive, she would say, "You witch, you have eaten my son!" That's what they would say. They would make that poor lady's life hell. That's why it was considered a blessing if a woman died before the husband as she didn't need to go through that pain. Otherwise, they would make her life even worse than hell, especially in India. Even until today, it is still like this in some villages. But nowadays society has evolved, so these things don't happen so often. Furthermore, if a child dies before the parents - but this is not because of somebody will blame them, but if a child dies before the parents it is also the curse of the parents.

Bhagavan Shankar says that, "This will not happen to the one who is surrendered to the Guru. The one who has the Grace of the Guru, the Guru will always protect."

Verse 146

Āyurārogyamaiśvarya
putra pautra pravardhanam
Akāmataḥ strī vidhavā
japān mokṣamavāpnuyāt

It grants longevity, health, wealth and power, children and grandchildren. If a widow repeats the Guru Gita without desire, she obtains salvation.

The *Guru Gita*, the praises of the Guru, the 'Song of the Guru' grants long life, "health, wealth and power." It "grants children and grandchildren." He says that you'll live long enough to see your grandchildren and not die young.

Lord Shiva said, "If a widow chants the *Guru Gita* without any desire inside of her, she obtains salvation, she shall be placed in the assembly of the saints."

Verse 147

Avaidhavyaṁ sakāmā tu labhate cānyajanmani Sarvaduḥkhabhayaṁ vighnaṁ nāśayecchā pahārakam

If she repeats it with a desire, she will not become a widow in her next life. It removes all misery, fears and obstacles and delivers one from curses.

If the widow repeats the *Guru Gita* with a certain desire in her heart, "in her next life, she will not become a widow." So here, even if the mantra is talking about being a widow, it doesn't mean literally widow, but it means a life of sadness and misery. Because very often people are so much focused on their misery that they are not free.

Here Bhagavan is saying that whoever chants the *Guru Gita*, their next life will be easy, happiness shall be upon them.

The *Guru Gita* "removes all misery, fears and obstacles and delivers one from curses." The *Guru Gita* protects one and assures one's true happiness. It even removes curses. Curse doesn't mean that someone utters a word saying, "Oh my Goodness! This person is bad, I shall curse this person! May he/she be born as a dog!" That can also happen, but here, in this verse,

Sarvaduḥkhabhayaṁ vighnaṁ nāśayecchā pahārakam, it means to remove the self-pity, the things which you put upon yourself, the things you create for yourself. And it gives protection from jealousy, for example. If you have something and somebody desires that so much, automatically, without the person willing it, there is jealousy which is created. And this jealousy can ruin somebody's life completely. That's what jealousy is. Jealousy has such a destructive power, which is so subtle that one doesn't notice it. Because one says, "It is a thought which has passed the mind", but jealousy is something deep, which comes out from the heart. When you are jealous, because you want to have something that other person has, automatically a certain darkness which is inside of you, goes to that person. Let's say, something good is happening to your life. For a long time you keep it inside of you, you didn't say anything. And one day you say it to your best friend. And your best friend says, "My God! That's really nice!" That's it! That's the end of your nice journey. Because even if the person didn't want to feel it, but the mind says, "I am jealous," due to that reaction, the energy, the vibration which leaves that person at that moment makes one fall. So automatically one loses that peace and happiness. Do you know how many people I have seen fall down due to that jealousy? Of course, both will bear the karma, the one who has the jealous quality and the one who is receiving. But the one who has created it will have to go through even more trouble than the one who received it. So, that's why jealousy is very subtle in itself. One has to be very cautious about what one lets out.

Bhagavan Shiva is saying that the one who is surrendered and chants the *Guru Gita* every day should not fear even that, because the Guru shields that person. The Grace of the Guru protects one from all kind of curses.

Verse 148

Sarva bādhā praśamanaṁ
dharmārtha kāma mokṣa dam
Yaṁ yaṁ cintayate kāmaṁ
taṁ taṁ prāpnoti niṣcitam

It overcomes all hurdles and grants four-fold fulfilment: righteousness, wealth, pleasure and salvation. Whatever desire its worshipper has is bound to be fulfilled.

The *Guru Gita* "overcomes all hurdles and grants four-fold fulfilment", so the *Guru Gita* fulfils, gives you "righteousness, wealth, pleasure and salvation."

In life it is said that one goes through four different stages. The first stage of life is Brahmacharya, when one goes through all the studies; you acquire the knowledge which will make you righteous and will give you a certain standard in life.

The second stage of life is Grihastha. The people who have taken the Grihastha life have to look after the family. They have to work night and day to meet the needs of their family, which means slavery. *[Swamiji and audience laugh]* No, not really. The quality of this stage of life is wealth.

The third stage is Vanaprastha. In this stage there is a change in your life towards spirituality and you find great pleasure in serving others, in serving the deity. You have more time – so mostly this happens after your retirement nowadays. So here He said, "When you retire, you have to develop this pleasure of serving the Lord."

Then, the fourth stage is Sannyas, which means to let go of everything and surrender completely to the Feet of the Lord. And that will bring you salvation.

Here Bhagavan Shankar is saying that these four gifts – righteousness, wealth, pleasure and salvation, are given to you just by reading and meditating on the Guru's Feet, form and name and singing His Glory; just by service to the Master.

"Whatever desire its worshipper has is bound to be fulfilled." Here Bhagavan Shankar is saying that whoever is surrendered to the Guru, whatever deep desire they have inside of them, it will be fulfilled, but according to the advancement of that bhakta. If the bhakta has a certain desire that will doom himself, that will never be fulfilled. But if it is a certain desire that will free oneself, the Guru will give full blessing for that.

Verse 149

Kāmitasya kāmadhenuḥ
kalpanā kalpa pādapaḥ
Cintāmaṇiś cintitasya
sarva maṅgala kārakam

The Guru Gita is the fabulous wish-fulfilling cow, Kamadhenu, to those who repeat it with desire, the wish-fulfilling tree to the imaginative type and the wish-fulfilling jewel to the contemplative. It is conducive to one's welfare in all ways.

The *Guru Gita*, the praises of the Guru "is the fabulous wish-fulfilling cow." So here He says that the praises of one's Guru is by itself Kamadhenu the cow which fulfils all the wishes.

"To those who repeat it with desire, the wish-fulfilling tree to the imaginative type, and the wish-fulfilling jewel to the contemplative. It is conducive to one's welfare in all ways." By the Guru's Grace, whoever has a certain desire, it shall be fulfilled. The one who wishes material things will get material things. The one who wishes spiritual achievement shall receive spiritual achievement. The one who desires wealth shall attain wealth. So the Guru makes everything happen according to one's dedication, one's awareness.

Verse 150

Mokṣa hetur japennityaṁ
mokṣa śriyamavāpnuyāt
Bhoga kāmo japedyo vai
tasya kāma phala pradam

He, who repeats it regularly to achieve liberation, becomes emancipated. He who repeats it with a desire for enjoyments would have his desire fulfilled.

"He, who repeats it regularly to achieve liberation, becomes emancipated." To the ones who wish *Moksha*, the Guru shall reveal to them the true *Mokshadham*, which is Vaikunta.

"He who repeats it with a desire for enjoyments would have his desire fulfilled." Here Bhagavan Shankar is saying that the *Guru Gita* carries the Grace to fulfil even the worldly desires of the devotee until one really realises what is the true desire in life.

Verse 151

Japecchāktaśca sauraśca
gāṇapatyaśca vaiṣṇavaḥ
Śaivaśca siddhidaṁ devi
satyaṁ satyaṁ na saṁśayaḥ

Let all worshippers of Shakti, of the Sun, of Ganapati, Vaishnavas and Saivites, recite the Guru Gita. There is not the least doubt that it yields fulfilment and success.

"Let all worshippers of Shakti, of the Sun, of Ganapati, Vaishnavas and Saivites recite the *Guru Gita*." Here Bhagavan Shankar is saying that all the five aspects of Hinduism, all of them must read the *Guru Gita*.

It is like that in all the traditions. They are all based on the importance of the Guru. Without the Guru they will not be led anywhere. All the five paths of Hinduism emphasise the importance of the Master in one's life. And before all the prayers, even before Ganapati, the prayers to the Master are a must.

"There is not the least doubt that it yields fulfilment and success." So if one wants to achieve spiritual success and fulfilment, it's a must to surrender to the Feet of the Guru.

Because if people say that the Guru is not important, and that they can reach there by themselves, they are in complete delusion. And in that delusion they don't only fall down themselves, but they also make others fall in it. And to make somebody else fall is considered to be one of the greatest sins.

Verse 152

Atha kāmyajape sthānaṁ
kathayāmi varānane
Sāgare vāsarittīre
athavā hariharālaye

Verse 153

Śakti devālaye goṣṭhe
sarva devālaye śubhe
Vaṭe ca dhātrīmūle vā
maṭhe vṛndāvane tath

Verse 154

Pavitre nirmale sthāne
nityānṣṭānato'pi vā
Nirvedanena maunena
japametaṁ samācaret

O Beautiful One! Now I shall speak about the spots where those with desires should recite the Guru Gita. It may be recited on the seashore, on a river bank, inside temples consecrated to Shiva or Vishnu or Shakti, in cowsheds, in all holy temples or ashrams, in the hollow of a banyan or thorn apple tree, or in Vrindavan. In any pure and clean spot, one should repeat it regularly in silence and with a serene and unagitated mind.

"O Beautiful One! Now I shall speak about the spots where those with desires should recite the *Guru Gita*." In the previous verses, Bhagavan Shankar has already spoken about the importance of the seat, colour and direction. Now He is talking about the importance of the spot, the place, for the ones who have a certain desire in their mind of attaining something in order to receive the full benefit.

"It may be recited on the seashore, on a river bank, inside temples consecrated to Shiva or Vishnu or Shakti." Here "...seashore, on a river bank..." means the flow of water. By the flow of water, the movement of water automatically creates a certain peace in a bhakta.

Meditating by the sea or by the river, the flow of the water element automatically helps one to go into a deep contemplative state because this element has a calming effect.

That's why the monasteries, the ashrams were always built by the rivers. Firstly because the land is fertile around the river, secondly there is constantly water, thirdly because near the bank of the river the energy itself is very calm. Fourthly because an ashram was built for beneficial reasons, for agriculture and so on.

So He says that by meditating also on these spots, one attains calmness, or peace.

Meditating, chanting the *Guru Gita* in the temples - the temples should be consecrated with an image of Lord Shiva, Vishnu or Shakti. These are the three main deities which are worshipped in the Hindu tradition: Devi, Shiva and Mahavishnu. Mahavishnu also includes Rama, Krishna and all the avatars of Mahavishnu. Shiva includes also Kartikeya, Subramanya, Ganesha, Santoshi and so on. And, of course, Devi includes all the aspects of Devi.

Do you remember when Narayana decided to be born as Lord Krishna on Earth, and He asked Yogamaya to manifest Herself in the house of Yashoda? At that moment Maha Devi said, "My Lord I am here to serve You. Whatever you wish, it is my command." At that moment Narayana blessed Devi by saying, "As people pray to Me in this world, you shall have as many temples as Me and your name should always be there to fulfil whatever is asked by the bhakta who comes to you." That's why the gopis run to Katyani aiming to get Krishna; and due to Katyani's blessing Lord Krishna agreed to do the Ras with them.

"In cowsheds, in all holy temples or ashrams," the cow is considered very holy in the Hindu tradition. It is considered to be the mother herself as she is always giving, she is always caring. That's why the cow is very dear to Lord Krishna.

"In the hollow of a banyan" tree. To have the full benefit of this mantra, one should go inside the banyan tree and chant it, or in a "thorn apple tree". He said that one should also go inside the thorn apple tree.

And above all He said, if you chant the *Guru Gita* in Vrindavan. This is Mokshadham, Vaikunta dham, Vrindavan dham. In Vrindavan it is the best of all. If you chant the *Guru Gita* and meditate on the Guru in Vrindavan, as Bhagavan Krishna said that there is no difference between the Guru and Him, you shall achieve the Supreme Lord Himself.

But in case it's not possible to go to Vrindavan, He said, "in any pure and clean spot, one should repeat it regularly in silence" with devotion "and with a serene and unagitated mind." It is very important to see what Bhagavan Shankar is saying there. He said that the *Guru Gita* should be chanted in silence, which means - here He is not talking only about the Glory of the Guru, He is talking about the Guru Mantra. The Guru Mantra should always be chanted in silence. The Guru Mantra should never by any means be chanted aloud. That's the secret the Guru Mantra holds.

And whenever you chant your Guru Mantra, you should be serene, you should be calm, not agitated or angry. Here He described how to chant the Guru Mantra, not in a harsh or quick way. No. He said that when you chant your Guru Mantra, even if you can't go to Vrindavan, you can bring Vrindavan to you. And how can you bring Vrindavan to you? It's by going inside of you, and by picturing yourself seated in Vrindavan. And then, there, inside of your heart, chant the Guru Mantra in a calm state, in a calm way.

Verse 155

Śmaśāne bhayabhūmau tu
vaṭamlāntike tathā
Siddhyanti dhauttare mūle
cūtavṛkṣasya sannidhau

One obtains siddhis by repeating it on a cremation ground, in frightful places, inside the hollow of a banyan or thorn apple tree, or under a mango tree.

Here Bhagavan Shankar is saying that by reciting the *Guru Gita* in the cremation ground one attains siddhis, one attains special gifts. Note one thing, siddhis awake due to one's spiritual advancement. The siddhis can also be a hindrance to the ones who don't put the Master first, but aim only for the siddhis and do everything just to get them. Just to get the siddhis doesn't mean anything! One can be born with many kinds of siddhis, but it doesn't mean that the person is great. What makes a person great is the love and dedication.

Here Bhagavan Shankar is saying that if one has love and dedication to the Master, and surrenders to the Master's Feet, all kinds of siddhis will be awakened, all kinds of siddhis will flow from the Master to the disciple. But the aim of such siddhis must also be clear. If these siddhis are used for personal gain, or to harm others, one will also bear the consequence.

If the *Guru Gita* is chanted "in frightful places" where there are ghosts or entities, like in a house which is possessed, by Guru's Grace the house will be freed from that possession.

If it is chanted "inside the hollow of a banyan or thorn apple tree, or under a mango tree," one attains different kinds of siddhis or different kind of gifts. For example, chanting the mantra in the banyan tree or under the banyan tree, one attains the siddhis of healing. If one chants it under a mango tree, one receives the Grace of speech.

If one chants the Guru Mantra, or the *Guru Gita*, in a place where you don't feel that there are good energies, that place will automatically be purified and changed, transformed due to the Grace of the Master. Note one thing - Guru Mantra should never be chanted aloud, always in silence.

Verse 156

**Guruputro varaṁ mūrkhas
tasya siddhyanti nānyathā
Śubhakarmāni sarvāni
dīksā vrata tapāṁsi ca**

'All good actions such as initiation, vows and penances, even of a fool who is devout and devoted to a Guru, bear fruit. Only a devotee would be successful.

Here Bhagavan Shankar is saying how important it is to be a bhakta who is surrendered to the Feet of the Master, who is surrendered completely to the will of the Master. They don't need to do anything. Just by concentrating on the Master's Form, by meditating on His Form, by meditating and chanting of His Name, they will attain everything! The ones who surrender as devotees to the Guru will be successful in their life.

There is this story of Trotakacharya. His name was Giri. Giri was a humble and devoted disciple of Adi Shankaracharya. And the duty, which was allocated to him, was to wash Adi Shankaracharya's clothes.

Adi Shankaracharya used to speak on the shastras, on the *Vedas*, on the *Puranas*, on the scriptures every day at a certain time. One day Giri was washing the clothes of Adi Shankaracharya. Then the class began and all the students, all the devotees of Adi Shankaracharya started running to listen to the class. While running to listen to the class, they were making fun of Giri, ridiculing him saying, "How foolish you are! You are washing the clothes of the Master while the Master is talking." Adi Shankaracharya noticed what was happening, so while Giri was washing the clothes, all the knowledge of the scriptures spontaneously flashed on his mind. This happened due to the Grace which was transmitted by Adi Shankaracharya to Giri. When this happened inside of him, he could not understand what was happening: how and why all of a sudden, he could chant the scriptures? So he ran quickly to the Feet of Adi Shankaracharya and as he opened his mouth, all the verses which the Guru had just explained about, came out of his mouth automatically. Even the most difficult verses, he could easily utter them. Seeing that, all the other students were shocked, "How come?" At that moment they realised that Guru seva is the most important thing. If the Guru had said to do something, one should not even think of something else, but should only do what the Guru had asked one to do.

There is a similar story in the life of Kabir. There was one incident in His life, when the disciples assembled together and asked Kabir, "Maharaj, please tell us who is Your greatest devotee?" Kabirji pointed to His son and said, "Kamal is My greatest bhakta, My true disciple." Everybody was wondering, "Why is Kabirji saying that

Kamal is His foremost disciple?" Kabir could read their minds. It was broad daylight, the sun was shining and He said to His son, "Kamal, I have dropped the needle, with which I was sewing. Can you please bring the lamp, so that I can look for it?" Straight away Kamal went, brought the lamp and gave it to the Guru. Kabirji didn't say anything. Then He asked his son, "Kamal, today some bhaktas, some devotees are coming and I would like you to cook some Prasad. Cook quickly some sweet ladoos, but instead of sugar put a handful of salt into them." Kamal did it without questioning. Meanwhile the others were observing how Kamal obeyed his Guru implicitly, without any questions. So, turning to the devotees Kabir said, "Don't you think that Kamal knew that My commands were ridiculous? Don't you think that he knew that cooking a sweet dish and putting salt in it would ruin it? Don't you think that he knew that the sun is shining and that I can see where the needle is? Yet he took the Guru's command without any questions."

So the moment one meditates, the moment one accepts without any question the command of the Guru, in that moment true meditation happens spontaneously. And by seeing such a dedication to the Guru, the Lord Himself gives Darshan to the bhaktas.

These are two stories which show that even a fool, who is dedicated to the Guru with full devotion, shall have everything. Even if one doesn't do much, yet just by having great reverence to the Master one shall get everything.

Verse 157

Saṁsāra mala nāśārthaṁ
bhava pāśa nivṛttaye
Guru gitāmbhasi snānaṁ
tattvajñaḥ kurute sadā

A knower of Truth always bathes in the waters of the Guru Gita to wash away his worldly impurities and become free from earthly temptations and snares.

Here Bhagavan Shankar is revealing to Goddess Parvati that if someone bathes in the waters of the *Guru Gita* - 'bathes' here means, if one's mind is surrendered, is submerged into the Love of the Guru, if someone's heart is full of the ocean of Love of the Guru, one gets rid of all impurities, one becomes free from earthly temptations, one attains liberation. Here He said, "How easy it is if one has devotion to the Guru! How easy it is if one just has love and without any questions follows the advice of the Master. And if one has such dedication, one attains the highest state of devotion!"

Such is the story of Guru Arjan who tested Bhai Manjh.

Bhai Manjh was a rich man who lived in a village which belonged to him. His devotional service was to look after the samadhi of his Guru, a saint by the name of Sakhi Sarwar. He didn't know anything else. His Guru had initiated him and he didn't know anything but his Guru Maharaj.

One day Guru Arjan, one of the Sikh Gurus, came to his village and gave a satsang. This satsang made a great impression on him, so he went to Guru Arjan and said that he wished to be initiated by him. As Guru Arjan had inner vision, He was omniscient, He asked Bhai Manjh who was the saint he was following at that moment. Bhai Manjh told Him, "I am following Sakhi Sarwar. My daily service is to take care of his samadhi." Seeing this devotion, Guru Arjan said to him, "I will initiate you."

Because sometimes when the Guru dies, He opens another door for the disciples in order to lead them to a higher level of spirituality. In spirituality, you can't just stay uniform in one level, but you always have to advance further. And the Master creates a certain situation that brings the disciples to where they really belong to. It was the same here.

Guru Arjan told him, "I will initiate you, but first you have to do one thing: go home, get rid of your puja room and then come back to me!" Because it was 'old'. You have to let go of the 'old' so that the 'new' can take over, no? If you don't let go of the old, how will the new do its work? It will not be possible! That's what Christ said, no? "You don't put new wine in an old barrel." Here it's the same! You have to empty the barrel completely, clean it. Then you can put 'new' wine inside.

So hearing the advice of the Master, he ran quickly to his place and started to knock the temple down. As he was doing that, everybody around him tried to discourage him, to demotivate him by saying, "Oh my goodness! What are you doing? By dismantling this temple you'll never be free. You'll get cursed." Then they were trying to pity him saying, "We would not like to be in your position." Bhai Manjh told them that was happy to follow the advice of his Guru and ready to suffer all consequences. His mind and heart had fully accepted Guru Arjan as his Guru. That's why he was again taking aadesh from a living Guru. By receiving the aadesh from the living Guru, this had more power than to keep following the deceased Guru. Because the living Guru always works accordingly with the deceased Guru. They go hand in hand. The past Guru had brought Bhai Manjh to a certain level, and the present Guru would bring him to another level. That's why Manjh knew the importance of following the advice of the Master without questioning.

After that, he returned to Guru Arjan. He blessed him

and initiated him with the Divine Name. He had passed the first test, but Guru Arjan wanted to test him further. Soon after his horse died. Then his cattle perished. Robbers broke into his house and stole everything. Of course, seeing all these unfortunate incidents, people started saying, "We told you! We warned you! By destroying your temple you would be cursed." Then, they advised him, "Go and build the temple back in your home!" But Manjh was not bothered at all. He told them that his Guru knew what was best for him and for all. Nothing could shake his faith in his Guru. Soon, he was completely ruined by successive misfortunes. In the beginning he was the landlord of the whole village and now he was reduced to such a state that he could not pay off his many debts. Finally people asked him to leave the village, while some of his 'friends' implored him to build the temple back in his place to ameliorate his whole situation. Everybody kept telling him, "Your Guru doesn't know anything! All the problems you have, all the pain that you are going through, it's due to the offence that you have done, by following what this Guru has told you to do." They all tried to discourage him and poison his mind.

In spite of all that happened, Manjh was determined to follow his Guru and with his family he had moved to another village. Before he was a wealthy man and didn't need to work, but now the time had come for him to learn something, to work and earn his own living. So he started to cut grass and sell it.

After a few months, Guru Arjan asked one of his disciples to bring a letter to Manjh with the following instruction, "Only give him the letter, after he gives you twenty rupees." So when the disciple reached the house where Manjh was staying, and Manjh saw the letter sent by his Guru, he was filled with love and joy. But as the Guru had said to the disciple who carried the letter to first receive the twenty rupees before he gives him the letter, how would he get the twenty rupees? Manjh didn't even have one penny. Then he took all the jewellery from his wife and sold it. He sold it all and made exactly the twenty rupees. He gave the disciple twenty rupees and received the letter. The moment he held in his hands the letter the Guru had sent, he went into deep ecstasy.

However, in order to test him further, his Guru sent one disciple to ask him to come and live in his ashram. So when Manjh heard about that, he rushed there with his family and took shelter in the ashram of Guru Arjan. The seva allocated to them in the ashram was to clean vessels in the kitchen and to take care of the firewood.

A few days later Guru Arjan wanted to test Manjh and said, "He is doing seva, but is taking food as payment. When one does true seva, one should not expect anything in return." As soon as he found out about these words of his Guru, he said to his wife that he didn't want anything in return for his service to his beloved Guru, who has given him the Guru Mantra, the most priceless gem.

Imagine how important the Guru Mantra was for Manjh! He realised the importance of the Guru Mantra. The Guru Mantra is not just a mantra which is plainly given. What one gets by receiving the Guru Mantra is priceless. That's why Meera said, "My Guru has given me the most precious gem in the form of the Mantra."

Since that day he started to cut wood in the forest during the night to sell it and buy food for him and his family. And during the day he continued doing seva in the kitchen of the ashram together with his family.

One night a violent storm broke out. This storm was very strong. The wind was so fierce that it blew everything. The wind was blowing so strongly that it blew Manjh into a nearby well, together with the wood that he was cutting. He fell into the well with the wood. So Guru Arjan, seated in the ashram, was fully aware of what was happening in the forest, so he asked some of his disciples to get a board and some rope and follow him to the forest.

When they reached the forest, the Guru said to one of the disciples, "Bai Manjh is at the bottom of this well. Shout down to him and tell him that we will lower a board tied to a rope. Tell him to cling to the board and we will pull him out." Then the Guru wanted to test him more, so he also added some words privately to one disciple, the one who was to call into the well. And he said to go and tell him this - so the man went to the well and call Bai Manjh, "Bai Manjh are you still around? Are you still alive?" Then, they heard, "Yes, I'm still alive." After hearing that, the disciple said, "We will send a board down with a rope, you cling to it and we will pull you out." Then the disciple said to Bai Manjh, "Brother, see the wretched condition you are in. And it is all due to the way the Guru has treated you. He has treated you in such a bad way, such a cruel way. That's why you are in such condition. Why don't you forget a Guru who does such things?" Here the disciple is trying to convince Bai Manjh saying, "Forget about that Guru. He is the bad one. He has done so many bad things to you. He has tested you in so many bad ways. You should forget about him! He's a bad Guru."

From down the well Bai Manjh replied, "Never! And as for you, ungrateful one, please never again speak so disrespectfully of the Guru in my presence. It makes me suffer agony to hear such shameful words." Here Bai Manjh, who is fully dedicated to his Guru, could not even bear one word of disrespect, one word of blasphemy towards his Guru. Nowadays people sit and talk bad things about their Guru and everybody will join and put their spice together. When somebody comes and tells, "Oh your Guru is like this, like this...," you keep listening, "Oh yes, He is indeed." This is the foolishness of Kali Yuga.

Manjh was very hurt by the disrespectful words, and he was very angry with that disciple.

Then the other disciple said to Manjh to catch hold of the board, but he insisted that the wood be pulled out of the well first. When Manjh was in the well, the wood was also with him. So instead of him going out, he said "No. Take the wood which I have collected for the fire for the Guru's kitchen first. It is for the Guru's kitchen, and I am afraid that it will get wet and not burn." That's what he said, "Take the wood first."

Finally Manjh was pulled out of the well. As he came out of the well, he came face to face with Guru Arjan. Seeing Guru Arjan in front of him, Guru Arjan addressed him saying, "My dear, you have gone through many trials and have met all of them with courage, faith and devotion to the Satguru." Here Guru Arjan praises - he reveals to his disciple that all this what he went through was just a test, a test of faith, courage and dedication to the Satguru. Guru Arjan asked Manjh, "Please ask for some gift or boons. Ask me whatever you want, I shall fulfil it. You have earned it and you deserve it. It will make me very happy to grant you whatever you ask." At that moment everybody would ask many things, no?

At this, Bhai Manjh fell on his knees before his beloved Master and with tears streaming down his cheeks, he exclaimed, "What boon could I wish for but you alone?" Here He said, "I don't wish for anything. What I wish, I wish for you, my Gurudev. Nothing else could ever be of any interest to me." Upon hearing these words coming from the heart of a true bhakta, coming from the heart of a true disciple, the Guru embraced Bhai Manjh and said, "Manjh is the darling of his Guru. And Guru is Manjh's only love." How wonderful it is that the Guru could say this to his disciple.

Manjh now, like the Guru, is a ship that carries people safely across the ocean of life and death. Here, just by the service, by dedication to Guru Arjan, Bai Manjh had been elevated to the same level as the Guru by the Grace of his Satguru. The Guru Himself has said to him, "You also shall be like me, carrying the people safely across the ocean of life and death." This is the Grace that the Guru gives to the one who is surrendered completely to him. So this is the story of Guru Arjan and Bai Manjh, where the true bhakta happily accepts everything, even the tests of the Guru. Not a single time he asked, "Why am I suffering so much? Why are all these calamities coming to me? But even when the Guru asked him to ask for a boon, his only wish was to serve only the Guru.

Kabir always prayed, "Give me the gift of devotion." That was the story of Guru Arjan and Bai Manjh which happened - I think - in the 17th century.

There are these praises of Kabir Das, "Give me the gift of devotion, O my Guru. Nothing else do I desire except Thy service day and night."

Jesus also said, "If one loves me and keeps my commandments, then they are my true disciples indeed." That's what Christ said, no?

The *Guru Gita* talks about this greatness - how a disciple must be. The disciples who are completely surrendered must forget about themselves and always place the Guru first.

So that's what the verse 156 says, that one may be "even a fool", an illiterate, but if one finds shelter at the Feet of the Master, the True Knowledge, not the knowledge which one hears or the book knowledge, but the True Knowledge shall flow spontaneously from the Master to the disciple.

Such was the life of Ragavendra Swami. Once Ragavendra Swami was passing by a shepherd. As the shepherd heard of him, he ran quickly and bowed down to Ragavendra Swami. He picked him up and asked, "My dear, what do you want?" The shepherd answered, "I would love to surrender myself at your Feet, but I am illiterate. I don't know how to read nor write. How can I serve you?" Hearing that, Ragavendra Swami closed his eyes, smiled and gave him the Guru Mantra, saying, "Chant Rama and Krishna's Name." From that moment, he became his disciple and Ragavendra Swami told him, "Stay here! Do your service to the cow. That will be my blessing to you. I shall be with you." So every day as he was bringing the cow for grazing, he would concentrate on Ragavendra Swami and chant his Guru Mantra.

One day, during the Mongol occupation, the king who was governing South India, Andhra Pradesh, was passing by on his horse. He was very proud and arrogant and he saw that the shepherd started to make fun of him, "Oh these Indians are all illiterate!" He was teasing him and saying to his people, "I will go and ridicule him." So he went there with his horse. He was well-known to be very cruel, especially to people of other religions. He started ridiculing the shepherd, saying, "If you don't know how to read, I shall decapitate you." The shepherd started to tremble saying, "I have never gone to school. I don't know how to write and read. And you want me to read this letter which is written in Sanskrit? Impossible!" At that moment the shepherd closed his eyes and thought of his Gurudev. He thought of Ragavendra Swami and he chanted, "Om Sri Ragavendraya Namaha" That's all He said! When he opened the letter, he could read everything in perfect Sanskrit. And he could explain everything even better than the scholars. The king was shocked and amazed, "How come? This shepherd, who is illiterate, explained the content of this letter better than a scholar. He lied to me for sure!" So he asked the shepherd, "So you know how to read! You are a great scholar! Who are you?" The shepherd said, "No. I don't know. What I've told you is true! I have never read anything! This is only due to my Gurudev's blessing. It's only due to Ragavendra Swami's blessing!"

Also during the Mongols occupation, Jiva Goswami had two disciples. And these two disciples used to be Muslims who worked in the court of king Akbar. The people there knew about them and at that time they were very simple people, they didn't had much knowledge. Later on they came into contact with Jiva Goswami and they got transformed. They had true knowledge about their spiritual path, where they belonged. So they left the court of king Akbar and surrendered to Jiva Goswami, taking shelter of him. After hearing that, the chief commander became very angry. He said, "These people have converted our people. We have to kill them." They rode their horses and reached Vrindavan. Hearing that the whole troupe was coming from Delhi to Vrindavan, the two disciples of Jiva Goswami said, "We don't want any harm to happen to our Guru. We don't want that our Guru suffers anything. So, we will go in front!" So what did they do? They took the blessing of Jiva Goswami and stood at the gate, waiting for them to come, saying "Okay, fine! We will give our lives if it's needed."

When the soldiers arrived, they also had great scholars with them. Whereas the two disciples were known to be simple-minded people without any proper education. First, the soldiers tried to convince them to change back to their former religion. Then a big discussion started happening and soon it became very philosophical, very scriptural. All the great scholars were asking these two disciples many questions. And all the answers were flowing out of their mouth automatically, spontaneously. At the end, the scholars were very convinced saying, "These two, we know them. They have never learned anything, but they have answered us all these questions, which even great scholars have never been able to answer. How is their Guru then?" At that moment, realising that there was a True Master in Vrindavan, they all returned back to Akbar's palace and revealed everything to him. Akbar was very impressed and consulted Birbal, his minister. Birbal, who was also a disciple of Jiva Goswami, but secretly, said, "Listen Akbar, Jiva Goswami is an associate of Bhagavan Himself. He is an associate of Chaitanya Mahaprabhu, who is the fusion of Radha and Krishna. Of course, by the blessing of such a person, even the dumb will start talking, the blind will see, the illiterate will have great knowledge." Such is the Grace of the Master to the one who is fully surrendered.

That's what this verse says, *Saṁsāra mala nāśārthaṁ bhava pāśa nivṛttaye*, "a knower of Truth". What is this

Truth? The Truth is that one must surrender to the Master without questioning, without having any doubt in one's mind, one shall become a true devotee, a true disciple.

Verse 158

Sa eva ca guruḥ sākṣāt
sadā sadbrahma vittamaḥ
Tasya sthānāni sarvāṇi
pavitrāṇi na saṁśayaḥ

He who is foremost amongst the knowers of the Absolute is, indeed, the Guru. There is no doubt that wherever he may live, that place becomes holy.

"He who is foremost amongst the knowers of the Absolute is, indeed, the Guru." In this verse Bhagavan Shankar is saying that the Guru, even if He appears not to know anything, in truth He is the best friend of the Ultimate. He knows the Ultimate as the Dear One. So if He knows the Ultimate, He has a good relationship with the Ultimate, "there is no doubt that wherever he may live, that place becomes holy". Here He said that wherever the Guru is, that place is sanctified. Because wherever the Guru is, His Dear One also stays with Him. And if His Dear One stays with Him, this means that wherever the Guru is, God is present, and that place is sanctified, it is blessed! Whoever goes into that energy, they are also imparted with that energy, with that blessing. And they themselves become holy. That's what Saint Augustine said - by being in touch with something which belongs to a saint, one is infused with the same saintliness.

Verse 159

Sarva śuddhaḥ pavitro'sau
svabhāvādyatra tiṣṭhati
Tatra devagaṇāḥ sarve
kṣetre pīṭhe vasanti hi

Wherever the supremely pure and taintless Guru stays, in natural course that whole region or abode comes to be inhabited by hosts of gods.

Here He says that where the Guru stays, the ashram where the Guru lives, it's not just the Guru that lives there. He says that the Guru becomes the pole that attracts all the devas there, too. He becomes the pole that attracts all the people who are longing for the Ultimate, longing for God Consciousness, longing for the Grace of the Master. He said that it's not only in the bhakta, but the transformation happens all around - the region itself gets transformed. For example, take

Springen. Six years ago, when we first moved here, when you were in the street, you would not even see one single person walking. Sometimes not even a fly. And nowadays, you see people everywhere, constantly, even in the middle of the night, at 2 o'clock, you see people walking around.

You see, the place where the Guru lives gets inhabited, not just by normal people, but by bhaktas, by devotees. And the devotees carry the blessing of the Master with them, which means wherever they go, they also sanctify the places. Nowadays if you go to Springen, it's not boring. It's very alive. So, like that even the hosts of gods are being pulled here. Maybe Maha Devi - She, in Her omnipresence, She is present everywhere. But in Her Swarupa - now we are celebrating Navaratri here! *[Swamiji is referring to the Navaratri Celebrations 2014]* In the Swarupa of Sri Krishna we celebrate Janmashtami. So all the devas had taken their abode in Shree Peetha Nilaya Itself. This is where they reside. This is where they live.

Verse 160

Āsanasthaḥ śayāno vā
gacchaṁstiṣṭhan vadannapi
Aśvārūḍho gajārūḍhaḥ
supto vājāgṛto'pi vā

Whether sitting in a posture, lying, moving around or standing, riding a horse or an elephant, asleep or awake, the Enlightened person is sanctified by his recitation of the Guru Gita. He would be free from the circle of rebirth and death.

Here He says that it doesn't matter which posture you take, whether you are lying down or you are awake, whether you are moving around or standing, or if you are dancing or driving a car, or you are riding a horse, whether you are asleep or awake. The ones who are meditating constantly on the Guru and chanting the *Guru Gita*, chanting the Guru's glory, meditating on the Guru's glory, meditating on the Guru within themselves, they are Enlightened.

You have to understand it clearly that the one who is surrendered to the Feet of the Master is not just a normal person. Someone who takes shelter at the Feet of the Master can't be just a simple person, because a simple person will find shelter somewhere else in the outside world. But the bhakta, the devotee, they must carry something great inside of them. Because it's not just by coincidence that one finds shelter at the Feet of the Master. It is due to great punya from previous lives, penance from previous lives, worship and dedication from many lives that one finds shelter at the Feet of the Master. This means that the bhaktas, the disciples are not simple people. They are the carriers of a certain blessing. That's what attracts them, otherwise they would not be attracted. The sense of belonging somewhere is there inside of them. The sense of surrendering is inside of them. And this doesn't happen just coincidentally, like you wake up, "Ah, puff! I am going to run to the ashram now!" No. It's a long life penance which has brought you to the Feet of the Master. Here He said that *supto vājāgṛto'pi vā*, those who take shelter at the Feet of the Master, you can assume that they will break free from the circle of birth and death.

Once there was a man. He went around the world searching for the perfect Guru. Wherever he went, he was very unfortunate, he could not find the perfect Master. They were greedy, they were fools, they were crazy and so on.

One fine day he had finally met one guru who met his expectations, who fulfilled all the qualities which he had in his mind. So one of his friends asked him (because he knew how he was), "How do you know that your guru is perfect?" So the man replied, "Oh, after talking to him, I came to that conclusion." So of course, the friend was wondering, "What did they talk about?" So the friend asked, "Please tell me! What did he tell you to convince you that he was the perfect guru?" Then the man said, "Well, he told me that I was the most perfect disciple in the world!"

Verse 161

Śucişmāṁşca sadā jñānī
guru gītā japena tu
Tasya darśana mātreṇa
punarjanma na vidyat

One who recites the Guru Gita is holy and wise, and merely by looking at him, you will be saved from rebirth.

Bhagavan Shankar is again reminding Devi saying that a true bhakta, who is surrendered to the Guru, who sings the praises of the Guru, who meditates on the Guru, is not merely just a simple person. They are not strange people as the world sees them. They are not fools. In reality it is the opposite. They are the wise ones because they have the knowledge of surrendering to the Feet of the Master. They carry the Grace of the Master with them, so whoever comes into contact with them, are also saved from this life. A bhakta, a true disciple, wherever they go they carry the blessing with them. And wherever the bhakta is, the Guru is ever-present with him/her. Here Bhagavan Shankar is saying that the world will point its finger not knowing what they have.

Once, Govinda Singh, who was a disciple of Guru Nanakji, asked him, "How important is the Guru?" Guru Nanak replied, "The more you are surrendered to the Guru, the more you will understand Him, the more you will perceive who He is."

Guru Nanakji gave a jewel to Govinda Singh and said, "Go to the market and ask several people what they would give you for this jewel. But don't sell it! You have to return it back to me." First he went to a flower seller. He showed her the jewel and asked, "How much would you give for this?" The flower seller looked at it and said, "Well, I shall give you one rupee for it." He replied, "Okay, fine!"

Then he went to a fruit seller who offered him three apples. The potato vendor told him, "I shall offer you ten bags of potatoes for that jewel." Afterwards, he went to a jeweller. The jeweller looked at the jewel thinking, "I can get this for my wife." So he said, "I will give you one thousand rupees for it." Govinda Singh replied, "No, I can't sell it. I have to give it back to my Guru." Then he decided to go to the best jeweller in town. This jeweller looked at the jewel, inspected it and said, "I shall give you 10 million rupees for that!" Of course, the disciple of Guru Nanakji was shocked, amazed. This jeweller got so impressed with the jewel that he went to the king and said, "There was a monk in the market trying to sell a very precious gem but he didn't sell it to me for 10 million rupees." The king ordered his guards to bring that monk. When Govinda Singh was brought to the presence of the king, the king looked at the jewel and said, "Do you know what you are holding here? I shall give you half of my kingdom for this jewel. This precious stone can transform any metal into gold. Where did you get it?" Govinda Singh said, "My Gurudev has given it to me. I asked him about the importance of the Guru. Then he gave me this jewel, and asked me to go to the market and ask several people the value of it. But my Guru also instructed me to not sell this jewel to anybody, and bring it back to him afterwards." At that moment the king realised that this was a test of the Guru for his disciple and said, "Go and take shelter at the Feet of the Guru who has given you this jewel! What your Guru has given to you is the Guru's Grace itself. And this is priceless!" This means that the mantra which the Guru gives is priceless! The Grace that the Guru bestows upon the disciple is priceless!

So that's what this verse stands for. The one who recites the *Guru Gita* automatically becomes holy and wise, and the source of salvation of others, because they carry with them this 'philosopher's stone'. And whoever touches that 'philosopher's stone' is also imprinted with that same Grace.

Verse 162

Samudre ca yathā toyaṁ
kṣīre kṣīraṁ ghṛte ghṛtam
Bhinne kumbhe yathākāśas
tathātmā paramātmani

Just as water merges in the ocean, milk in milk, butter in butter, the space inside a broken pot in the space outside, the individual soul merges in the Universal Being.

Bhagavan Shankar is saying that whoever surrenders to the Feet of the Master, whoever meditates and chants the *Guru Gita*, they become One with the Master. The more dedicated they are to the Master, the more the Light of the Master shines through them. That's what Christ said to His disciples, "Go! To those who you bless, they shall be blessed. To those who reject the blessing, the blessing will be taken away. I send you!" Because when He sent His disciples, He blessed them. You see, the blessing is not just, "Oh the Master has lifted his hand and put it on the head and finished!" No. The infusion of the energy on the disciple, on the bhakta, on the devotees, means that the Guru always places Himself in front of the disciple. So when the disciples bless, in reality it's not them who are blessing, it's the Master who is blessing. That's the blessing Christ has given to His disciples. He said, "Whoever remembers Me and does the service in My Name, I shall be among them." So He has given this blessing! Two thousand years ago He said, "Eat this bread! This is my body. Drink this wine! This is my blood. And whoever eats and drinks of that shall not perish!" So He has blessed the disciples to carry on with that lineage from that moment on. This means that through the blessing the Master always places Himself in front of his disciples, and in the disciples, until there is no difference between the disciples and the Guru. The same as in the story of Guru Arjan and his bhakta Bai Manjh.

But it's sometimes difficult to reach that level because it takes complete surrender. Sometimes even to those who are blessed with the Divine vision, if they don't realise the Grace which the blessing of the Master carries, they don't fully reach the Ultimate. Even if the Supreme Himself has given them the vision, this doesn't mean that they will attain Him. Out of mercy the Lord can give a vision to someone due to past life experiences but that doesn't mean anything! Without the blessing of the Master all this is in vain. With the blessing of the Master one becomes similar to the Master. That's what

Bhagavan Shankar said, *Bhinne kumbhe yathākāśas tathātmā paramātmani* - one attains the Supreme through the Grace of the Master. This is clearly shown in one story of the life of the saint Namdev Maharaj.

Namdev Maharaj was a well-known saint from Maharashtra and a great devotee of Panduranga Vittala. Since childhood he had been blessed with a vision of Lord Panduranga, so he used to sit and talk with Krishna. Due to that great fortune, he started to consider himself as someone special because the Lord every day used to come to him, talk to him and eat with him. So he became very proud and would walk looking at everybody else under the nose. I would call it 'arrogance française'. *[Swamiji says this with an affected tone of voice and the audience burst out laughing]*

So one day, Lord Panduranga wanted to test him, wanted to get rid of all this negativity from his dear one. And he wanted to humble him, he wanted him to realise the importance of the Grace of the Guru. So Bhagavan decided that Namdev Maharaj needed a Guru. There was a feast in the village of Pandharpur. This feast was arranged by the potter-saint Gora. Gora arranged a big party and all the saints around were invited and each one there would be tested by Gora.

Saint Dnyaneshwar, who is another saint from Maharashtra, a saint from Alandi asked Gora to test each of the 'pots' to see which ones were fully baked in the Knowledge of the Supreme Reality. So they were all asked to sit in a long line. As they were sitting, Gora went around and hit each one of them on the head with a stick, to see if each one is well-baked. Everyone was very humble, they all submitted to this, but only Namdev was arrogant and refused - pride, he refused to be hit by Gora, because he was thinking, "How dare Gora, who is a potter, to hit him?" So all the saints, seeing this pride inside of him, started laughing at Namdev saying, "You are 'half-baked'." As they were all laughing and mocking him, he felt very embarrassed.

So he ran to Panduranga to comfort him. The Lord appeared in front of him, comforted him and told him that unless he attained Enlightenment, he would not understand why the saints were laughing at him. That shocked Namdev because he thought he was very special, he thought he was very wise, he thought he was very dedicated. Lord Panduranga Vittala said to him, "You are not Enlightened! Even if you have seen the Lord, you have not yet reached Enlightenment." And due to that 'unenlightenment' he could not understand why the saints were laughing at him.

Panduranga said to Namdev to go to a certain saint by the name of Vishoba Kechara, who was staying in a Shiva temple on the outskirts of the village. Listening carefully to Vittala, Namdev reached there. He entered the temple and saw an old man lying down with his feet resting on the Shiva Lingam. What a big sacrilege! *[Audience laughs]* Namdev very arrogantly clapped his hands to wake up the old man. Vishoba woke up, looked at Namdev and said, "Oh, you are that Namdev who Vittala has sent, aren't you?" Namdev was shocked and thought that this man must be a great being. Because he was also talking to Vittala, Panduranga. Then Namdev said, "You seem to be a great man, but why are you resting your feet on the Shiva Lingam?" Then the shocked man said, "Oh, are they on the lingham?" Then the old man said, "Please remove them for me. I am very tired. I can't lift my feet." Namdev lifted the old man's legs and placed them somewhere else, on a certain spot. But the moment the feet of the old man touched the floor, a Shiva Lingam appeared on the spot. Wherever he would place the feet of the old man, at that spot a Shiva Lingam would appear. Finally, Namdev took the old man's leg in his lap. The moment he put the old man's leg in his lap he entered deep samadhi. He entered the state of Shiva Tattva. At that moment he attained the knowledge of a great bhakta, because Lord Shiva is the greatest bhakta of Narayana Himself. You see, first he was always putting the feet of the old man everywhere until he surrendered to the feet of the old man as the Guru. Only then he took the feet in his lap. Taking shelter at the Feet of the Enlightened one, the saint touched him and gave him Enlightenment. He didn't do much. Only when this pride, this arrogance has been removed, that true Enlightenment automatically awakened inside of him.

Then Vishoba Kechara asked him, "Go back to the village!" Namdev returned to his house and he stayed at home. Noticing that Namdev Maharaj was not coming to the temple anymore, the Lord Vittala Himself went to see him and asked him, "Why are you not coming to the temple?" Namdev replied, "Where is it that You are not, my Lord? And can I exist in any way apart from You? And it is only through Your Grace, through the Grace of the Guru that I have come to that Enlightenment: that you are not just seated there in the temple, but you are seated everywhere. And such Enlightenment comes only by the Grace of the Lord in the form of the Guru."

So this was how Saint Namdev attained Enlightenment. Even if he was born as a saint, yet he needed a Guru.

The story is similar to the one of Sukadev Maharaj.

Sukadev was the son of Veda Vyasa, the one who compiled the *Vedas*, the *Puranas*, the *Srimad Bhagavatam*, the *Gita*. Sukadev was the one who revealed the *Srimad Bhagavatam* to king Parikshit before he got bitten by the snake and died.

Veda Vyasa's son was very knowledgeable due to previous births, previous samskaras. He had the whole knowledge already inside the womb of his mother. As a child he used to spend all of his time meditating in the forest near his father's ashram.

Saint Sukadev was ever-free. One day, while he was meditating, a desire arose in his mind to go to Vaikunta to see Lord Vishnu. When he reached there, the gatekeepers Jaya and Vijaya informed Lord Vishnu of who had come to visit him, but Mahavishnu didn't allow him to come inside. They went back outside to inform Sukadev about it and said, "We are very sorry, but you have no Guru and those without a Guru can never enter Vaikunta." Bhagavan Vishnu nor the guardians themselves didn't allow Sukadev to enter Vaikunta. Such a great sage's son, such a great yogi was not allowed into Vaikunta because he didn't have any Guru.

Suka returned to his father and said to him what had happened. He was a bit vain and proud, thinking that he was the son of a great Rishi, and he had already done so many years of tapas, so there was no need of a Guru. Due to that he was very proud and arrogant thinking, "What's the use of having a Guru. I have already done so many tapas. And I am great. I was born already great. However, Bhagavan Vishnu Himself had said that a Guru was necessary, so Suka asked Vyasa Dev to advise him who shall be his Guru. His father, Veda Vyasa said, "There is only one Guru for you and that is King Janaka of Videha." King Janaka was Sita's father. This shocked

Sukadev and he said to his father, "Father, have you lost your mind? What is there in common between a king and a sannyasin? He was shocked. He was a sannyasin and the king had to rule a whole kingdom, so he was not detached, he was not free. How could a king advise a sannyasin? So he was shocked. That's why he said to the father, "Have you gone mad?" Suka carried on saying, "How can I take him as my Guru?" Veda Vyasa said, "There is nobody else who could be your Guru."

With a strictness Veda Vyasa sent Suka to King Janaka twelve times, and twelve times he returned even before reaching there, before reaching the palace due to doubts and misgivings inside his mind. Once he even reached the palace, but on seeing the richness of the palace and the great assemblage of worldly people, he thought that the king must be one who is given up to sensual pleasure, and so he was not prepared to accept him as his Master.

Inside his mind more doubts and suspicions arose. The more doubts and suspicions one has about a Realised Soul, the more one harms oneself. So He said here that the more you doubt a Realised Soul - you are not harming that Realised Soul, in reality you are harming yourself. Suspecting or slandering a Mahatma destroys one's merits (punya). You have acquired great merit to be born as a human being, to reach the level of human so that you can attain the Divine, but by slandering or talking bad of a Master one loses all punya and one dooms oneself to the lower level of Consciousness.

When Suka was being sent back to the king for the thirteenth time, sage Narada took pity on him. Narada Muni disguised himself as an old brahmin and was carrying a basket of earth on his head. As he approached a small river which was flowing nearby, he would throw the earth into it and it would get washed away. Seeing this, Suka approached him and said, "Look here, old man. First put some sticks across the stream and then some large lumps of earth on them and then only throw the earth on that. Otherwise it will be only fruitless labour if you are trying to build a dam across the river the way you are doing it."

So Narada said, "I am only losing my day's effort. But there is a young man who is a bigger fool than I am, and he is Suka Deva, the son of Veda Vyasa. For he has already lost twelve of the fourteen merits that he possessed. Here, Narada in disguise said to Sukadev, "You are a fool! Due to past lives you have acquired fourteen merits, punya. But due to not accepting king Janaka as your Guru, you have already lost twelve merits from that. You have only two left." When Suka heard that he had already lost twelve of his fourteen merits, he fainted out of shock. *[Swamiji says this in a joking way and the audience laughs]* When he regained consciousness, he was all alone, but he remembered the words of the old man and rushed to the king's palace.

Still having some pride that he was the son of Veda Vyasa, he thought that the king would come and meet him on the way. But no one came to meet him. When the king was informed of his arrival, he gave the orders, "Let him stand right where he is." Suka just happened to be standing on the spot where the palace garbage was thrown over the wall. Poor Suka! And as a result, it was not long before he was buried under all the rubbish.

Four days passed in this way, so when the king enquired, "What happened to Suka who had come to see me?" "He has been standing in the same place, Maharaj," replied the servant. So the king ordered, "Let him be extricated from the heap of rubbish, bathed, dressed and brought here."

King Janaka, knowing that Suka was proud of his renunciation, created an illusion. Just after Suka entered the room, a servant came running in with a report that the entire town was on fire. "It's all God's Will," said Janaka cooly. After a short while another report came that all of the king's courts were reduced to ashes. "God's Will," said the king. Then the news came that the king's own palace was on fire. "All God's Will," repeated the king. Suka was thinking what a fool the king was not to do anything about the fire. Suka grabbed his bag and started to run away to save himself from the approaching fire. But, as Suka was running, the king said, "Where are you going?" And he got hold of Suka's arm. "Look," said the king, "all of my wealth and possessions have been burnt to ashes, but I haven't bothered about them. Now that the fire has reached the palace, you have taken hold of this small bundle of your possessions with the intention of saving them. After all, what are your things worth? Now, who exactly is the greater renunciant - you or I?" Suka realised that the king was a true renunciant and sought initiation from him, but the king said, "You do not deserve it."

Now the king ordered that a great festival be held in honour of Suka's visit to the city. Festivities, dances, plays and various stalls were set all around. All was to entertain Suka. When everything was ready, the king asked Suka, "Go around, enjoy all that have been brought here for you, but take this pot of milk and carry it with you." Then he asked the soldiers to accompany him, "Take Suka through every part of the city. Let him see everything and miss nothing. But if he should spill a single drop of milk from this cup, my orders are that you should behead him on the spot." Poor Suka!

Suka went out with the soldiers and came back in the evening. "I am sure that you had a nice day? How did you enjoy everything?" The king asked Suka. Suka said, "O king, as it turned out, I saw nothing!" The King asked, "What? You didn't see anything?" So Suka didn't see anything! He was so concentrated on carrying the milk fearing that his head would be removed. *[Swamiji says this in a joking way and the audience laughs]* Then king Janaka said, "Suka, that is how I live in the midst of all this luxury and grandeur. I see nothing. For at every moment my thoughts are centered on the Lord lest I too should lose my life," said the king.

How wonderful it is! Janaka's mind was focused on the Supreme Lord Himself at all time. He was doing his duty as a king, but his mind was always focused on the Lord, fearing that he would lose his life. That's what Christ said, "It's easier for a camel to enter a hole of a needle than for a rich person to enter the kingdom of heaven."

So here the king Janaka said, "Imagine that the cup is death, the milk is your mind, and the festivities are the outside pleasures and splendours of the world. I pass through this world with great caution, so that the milk of the mind is not spilled, or agitated, and all attention is concentrated every moment on the Supreme Lord. For even a moment spent in not thinking of Him would be death to me." The king could now see that Suka's mind was cleansed of pride and was ready to be initiated. So then king Janaka initiated him.

This story is very meaningful. He, Janaka, who had everything as a king, but yet his mind was always focused on the Lord Himself. It was never diverted from his aim.

Verse 163

Tathaiva jñānī jīvātmā
paramātmani līyate
Aikyena ramate jñānī
yatra tatra divāniśam

In the same way, the enlightened person's individuality is merged in God. He revels in the bliss of the Self, day and night, wherever he is.

The *Guru Gita* gives to a bhakta the taste of the Lord Himself. He awakens this Amrit, this Divine nectar of the Guru, and makes one be in the blissful state, night and day. Remembering the Guru doesn't mean to plainly remember Him, but one should remember Him with Love, and when one remembers Him with Love, only then true bliss will be awakened from within oneself.

Verse 164

Evaṁ vidho mahāmuktaḥ
sarvadā vartate budhaḥ
Tasya sarva prayatnena
bhāva bhaktiṁ karoti yaḥ

Verse 165

Sarva sandeha rahito
mukto bhavati pārvati
Bhukti mukti dvayaṁ tasya
jihvāgre ca sarasvatī

Thus, a wise being always dwells in supreme freedom, serving God tirelessly and with deep devotion. O Parvati! He becomes emancipated, without a doubt. He enjoys material prosperity as well. Saraswati (the Goddess of Speech) dwells on the very tip of his tongue.

"Thus, a wise being always dwells in supreme freedom," Here Bhagavan Shankar is saying that the wise one, the one who is a true bhakta, a devotee who has surrendered to the Guru's Feet always dwells in the Supreme Freedom, because one becomes like a child. A child doesn't bother about anything. The parents are the ones who have to care and look after the welfare of the children. So, here He said that a bhakta dwells in the Supreme Freedom because for the one who is fully surrendered, there is the guarantee that at the end of this life they will be free.

"Serving God tirelessly and with deep devotion. O Parvati! He becomes emancipated, without a doubt. He enjoys material prosperity as well. Saraswati (the Goddess of Speech) dwells on the very tip of his tongue." Here Bhagavan Shankar is saying that those devotees who are surrendered to the Guru, due to Guru's Grace, have the Goddess of Speech, Vagdevi, Saraswati Devi seated on the tip of their tongue. That's why bhaktas, who are fully surrendered to the Feet of the Master, whatever they say, even if they proclaim a curse upon somebody, that person will be cursed. And if they proclaim a blessing upon someone, that person will be blessed.

That's what Christ said, "To those who you bless, they shall be blessed. To those who you curse, they shall be cursed." Because to the bhakta who is fully surrendered, the Guru and the bhakta become One.

Verse 166

Anena prāṇinaḥ sarve
guru gītā japena tu
Sarva siddhiṁ prāpnuvanti
bhuktiṁ muktiṁ na saṁṣayaḥ

There is no doubt that all who recite in prayer the Guru Gita will obtain all the siddhis, accomplishments, pleasures, wealth and liberation.

"There is no doubt that all who recite in prayer," with devotion and love "the *Guru Gita* will obtain all the siddhis", all the Grace, all the gifts, "all accomplishments, pleasures, wealth and liberation." Bhagavan Shankar is saying that a bhakta should not doubt that it is possible to reach there. The aim of the bhakta is to attain the Grace of the Master, the Guru Kripa. And with the Guru Kripa one is elevated and obtains all the gifts, all accomplishments, all wealth, even liberation.

Verse 167

Satyaṁ satyaṁ punaḥ satyaṁ
dharmyaṁ sāṅkhyaṁ mayoditam
Guru gītāsamaṁ nāsti
satyaṁ satyaṁ varānan

O Beautiful One, whatever I have said is true religion, True Knowledge. It is true, absolutely true that there is nothing like the Guru Gita.

"O Beautiful One, whatever I have said is true religion, True Knowledge." Here Shiva is saying that true religion is surrendering to the Guru's Feet! It's not about the dogmatism of the outside, but true religion lies at the Feet of the Master. And that's True Knowledge because only the Master's Feet give the knowledge of the Self.

"It is true, absolutely true that there is nothing like" the praises of the Guru. There is nothing else greater than surrendering to the Feet of the Master.

Verse 168

Eko deva ekadharma
eka niṣṭhā paraṁtapaḥ
Guroḥ parataraṁ nānyan
nāsti tattvaṁ guroḥ param

One God, one religion and one faith are the highest austerity. There is nothing higher than the Guru. There is no tattwa more significant than the Guru.

Bhagavan Shiva is saying that there are no qualities in a bhakta which are higher than the Guru's own qualities inside the bhakta. There is only one God, one religion. There is only one faith and that's "the highest austerity", the highest sadhana, the highest realisation! If one by oneself tries to attain that level, it's very difficult! Because one doesn't see oneself as an emanation of Everything. One doesn't perceive oneself being present everywhere. Whereas the Guru perceives Himself not limited by the physical only. He perceives it is Him who is seated inside everything, everywhere. That's why Lord Shiva refers to the Guru as "one God, one religion and one faith". One religion: this is the dharma, the discipline; one faith is the submission, the love; and only one God is the Ultimate Himself as the Guru.

Verse 169

Mātā dhanyā pitā dhanyo
dhanyo vaṁśaḥ kulaṁ tathā
Dhanyā ca vasudhā devi
gurubhaktiḥ sudurlabhā

Fortunate is the mother of the one devoted to the Guru, fortunate is his father. Blessed is his family; blessed, indeed, are his ancestors. Fulfilled is the earth, O Goddess, on which he walks, as devotion to the Guru is so rare.

"Fortunate is the mother of the one devoted to the Guru." Here He said, "Because a bhakta is not a normal person. A disciple is not just a normal person. He said, "Blessed is the mother of that disciple." And fortunate is his father due to having a child who has fully surrendered to the Feet of the Master. If such a child was born to them, this means that they also have good punya from past lives. Because such a soul can't be born in just a normal womb.

Bhagavan Krishna said in the *Gita* (Chapter 6, verse 42) that each one is born in the womb of the mother according to the punya of the past. If one has the sattvic quality, the merit is also sattvic, so automatically they will be born to a family which makes it easy for them to go on a spiritual path, to follow a way to attain the Divine.

He also said, "Blessed is his family; blessed, indeed, are his ancestors." Here He didn't say only the family, because if one goes on the spiritual path and dedicates the life to the Feet of the Master, not only they are blessed, but the parents are blessed, the family is blessed, and the ancestors are also blessed, so the whole generation is freed. That's why when we do Pinda we invoke the whole generation, not only the intimate or the knowing ones. No. But also the ones who you don't know, from your generation, from that lineage to which your family comes from – they all get blessed.

"Blessed, indeed, are his ancestors. Fulfilled is the earth, O Goddess, on which he walks, as devotion to the Guru is so rare." Here He said that the one who has devotion to the Guru, a true bhakta is rare. That's why it is said that disciples, Christ had only twelve, but he had many devotees. But even among the disciples, only one was truly, fully, completely devoted to Him. That's why I can say that it's true what Bhagavan Shankar is saying here. It's indeed very rare to have a disciple who is completely surrendered to the Guru. Because very often, it appears only as surrendered. But here Bhagavan Shankar is saying that the mind and the heart have to be completely surrendered.

Verse 170

Śarīram indriyaṁ prāṇāś
cārthaḥ svajanabāndhavāḥ
Mātā pitā kulaṁ devi
gurureva na saṁśayaḥ

There is no doubt, O Goddess, that the Guru is the body, the senses, the prana, the most precious wealth, all the near and dear ones. He is the father, the mother, the entire family, in fact.

Here Bhagavan Shankar is saying that once you met your Satguru, your Satguru becomes everything to you. The Satguru becomes the mother, the father, the family. The Satguru Himself becomes your own body. The Satguru Himself becomes the breath of yourself, the senses. You have to perceive that the Guru is indeed the One who is fully inside of you.

That's why at the beginning of the *Guru Gita* (commentary of verse 35) I said that when in India they asked you, "Who is your father?" especially if you are on the spiritual path, you should always say that the Guru is the father, the Guru is the mother and the Guru is the family. Because there is no mother, father or anybody else who can lead you to the Ultimate, but the Guru.

A mother can give you the physical body. What else can a mother do? Look after you? This is the parents' duty. They can't escape that duty. The duty of the father is to provide for the family. But the Guru can lead you to the highest state. The mother can't give you God Consciousness. The father can't give you God Consciousness. Only the Guru can give you that! Only the Guru can give you the Grace of the Supreme. That's why to the one who is fully surrendered the Guru is the mother, the father and the Guru is everything!

Verse 171

Ākalpa janmanā koṭyā
japavrata tapaḥ kriyāḥ
Tat sarvaṁ saphalaṁ devi
guru santoṣa mātrataḥ

O Goddess! All merit acquired by the repetitions of mantras, fasting, austerities and other scriptural disciplines practised for aeons, or for millions of births, is obtained just by pleasing the Guru.

Here He said that one can do lots of penance, lots of sacrifices, one can have many forms of discipline in one's life, but just by pleasing the Guru one acquires all the merits.

There was a man who went to a Guru. He wanted some instructions for his life. The Guru told him, "Thou art That." This is what every Guru says, no? "You are That! You are the Ultimate!" The man wasn't satisfied with these words, so he decided to look for another Guru. That Guru looked at him and understood all the desires that he had in his mind. He saw on which level he was. So the Guru said, "I can't instruct you just like that! What would you do with it? You have to work hard to receive a certain initiation. You have to be worthy of that initiation." At that moment that man was ready to do whatever the Guru would ask him. The instruction of the Guru was, "Shovel cow dung for twelve years." Nothing else. Twelve years later, the Guru Himself called the disciple and told him the same which the first Guru had said, "Thou are That." But this time, when the Guru said, "You are That," the disciple was infused with That! The disciple was infused with God Consciousness! He got awakened. He had the Divine awareness, he realised the Supreme within himself. He attained God-Realisation instantly.

That's why one must be ready! The ones who are fully surrendered to the Feet of the Master don't think of themselves. They don't aim something as self-gratification. Whatever they do is for the sake of the Master.

That's why He said in this verse *Ākalpa janmanā koṭyā*

japavrata tapaḥ kriyāḥ Tat sarvaṁ saphalaṁ devi guru santoṣa mātrataḥ - just by the *santoṣ* of the Guru, what one may give it to the disciple just by a glance itself. And this is true, actually!

Verse 1/2

Vidyā tapo balenaiva
manda bhāgyāśca ye narāḥ
Gurusevāṁ na kurvanti
satyaṁ satyaṁ varānane

Verse 1/3

Brahma viṣṇu maheśāśca
devarṣi pitṛ kinnarāḥ
Siddha cāraṇa yakṣāśca
any'pi munayo janāḥ

O Beautiful One! It is true, undoubtedly true, that those who do not serve the Guru are unfortunate, even with their learning power gained through austerities and the strength. Brahma, Vishnu, Shiva, divine seers, ancestors, kinnaras, siddhas, yakshas, charanas and other sages could attain their respective states only through devotion to the Guru.

Here Bhagavan Shiva Himself is saying that all the Trimurti, all the kinnaras, all the siddhas, all the saints, rishis, sages, they have attained that level, where they are, only due to the Grace of their Guru. Only due to the Grace of their Guru as Shriman Narayana Himself they have attained that level. They are in the Grace of the Master. What for the ones who do not serve the Guru? How unfortunate they are! How miserable their life is. Even if they are well-educated and have all knowledge, their knowledge is only book knowledge. And this kind of knowledge drags them deeper and deeper into the forest of delusion. Here Bhagavan Shiva is saying that the ones who serve the Guru are blessed because they don't need to do much. The Guru takes care of them! The Guru serves them! The Guru looks after their welfare! And the Guru aims the highest for His disciple.

Verse 174

Guru bhāvaḥ paraṁ tīrtham
anyatīrthaṁ nirarthakam
Sarva tīrthāśrayaṁ devi
pādāṅguṣṭhaṁ ca vartate

Devotion to the Guru is the most sacred abode. All other holy places are of no consequence. O Goddess, all centres of pilgrimage, in fact, lie in the Guru's feet, nay, just in one of his toes.

Guru bhāvaḥ paraṁ tīrtham - "Guru is the most sacred abode". The most sacred place for a bhakta is at the Feet of the Guru. The most sacred abode where Shriman Narayana Himself resides is the heart of the Guru.

anyatīrthaṁ nirarthakam sarva tīrthāśrayaṁ devi pādāṅguṣṭhaṁ ca vartate - "All other holy places are of no consequence. O Goddess, all centres of pilgrimage, in fact, lie in the Guru's feet, nay, just in one of His toes." Here Bhagavan Shiva said that all the pilgrimage places lie at the Feet of the Master. Then He said, "No. Not at the Feet, but just the toe of the Master" holds all the pilgrimage places. So imagine when you go on a pilgrimage with the Master! How much punya is it?

Verse 175

**Japena jayamāpnoti
cā nanta phalamāpnuyāt
Hīnakarma tyajan sarvaṁ
sthānāni cā dhamāni ca**

Repetition of the Guru Gita brings infinite rewards including victory. But one who recites it should discard all unworthy actions and detestable places.

Bhagavan Shiva has instructed before that the place where one recites the *Guru Gita* must be a calm place (commentary of verses 152-154). While reciting the *Guru Gita*, when one sits down and meditates on the Guru, one should put a certain discipline in oneself in order to receive the full reward of it, the full blessing of it. One should learn to control the mind and not let the mind wander around. When one recites the *Guru Gita*, only the Guru should be in the mind of that bhakta! Only the praises of the Guru must be on the lips of that bhakta. In each breath of the bhakta, only the name of the Guru shall echo.

Verse 176

Japaṁ hīnāsanaṁ kurvan
hīnakarma phala pradam
Guru gītāṁ prayāṇe vā
saṅgrāme ripusaṅkaṭ

Verse 177

Japañ jaya mavāpnoti
maraṇe muktidāyakam
Sarva karma ca sarvatra
guruputrasya siddhyati

Japa on an improper seat, asan, and trivial actions bear poor fruit. Repeating Guru Gita while undertaking a journey or facing danger from the enemy on the battlefield would give victory. He attains salvation if he recites it at the time of death. All his effort, wherever he may be, would be successful.

Here Bhagavan Shankar is reminding one that if you do "japa on an improper seat, asan, and trivial actions bear poor fruit". Your state of mind is very important while you're meditating on the Guru. He said that if your mind is diverted, if you are not seated properly, if you are not relaxed, if you are not focused, the fruits will also be in accordance to that. Whereas if you are seated fully absorbed in reciting the *Guru Gita*, then you will receive the blessing. Whatever you sow, you shall reap.

"Repeating *Guru Gita* while undertaking a journey or facing danger from the enemy on the battlefield would give victory." Here it doesn't mean that you are on the battlefield and then you start looking for your book to start chanting the *Guru Gita*. No. The *Guru Gita* stands for the Guru Mantra, the connection with the Guru. This blessing of the Guru is ever with you. Wherever you go, the Guru is with you. In whatever danger you are, the Guru is with you.

The bhakta "attains salvation if he recites it at the time of death." If one chants the Guru Mantra at the time of leaving this body, for sure they will be liberated. And I can assure you of that!

"All his efforts, wherever he may be, would be successful." Whoever chants the *Guru Gita* by the Grace of the Guru, wherever one is, it doesn't matter in which corner of this world one is, the Guru is seated in the heart of that person. The Guru is never far away from a true bhakta. The Guru is inside the heart observing everything. Babaji - Satya Narayan Das, calls it the 'hidden camera, *Chitragupta*.' When we were in Kenya, Babaji talked about Chitragupta - it was really funny! 'Chitra' means picture, 'gupt' means cave, so Chitragupta is the one who is taking pictures from inside *[Swamiji bursts out laughing]* and keeps a recording, the 'hidden camera'. So the 'hidden camera' is not out there, it's inside. So the inner Guru is not there, but He is inside of you.

Verse 178

**Idaṁ rahasyaṁ no vācyaṁ
tavāgre kathitaṁ mayā
Sugopyaṁ ca prayatnena
mama tvaṁ ca priyātviti**

O, the one so near to me! Do not disclose the mystery that I have revealed to you. Make every effort to keep it as a secret.

Bhagavan Shankar is saying that this secret should not be disclosed to anyone. The secret of the Guru is only for the bhakta, for the disciple, and they should treasure it. It should not be revealed to anyone who is not worthy. Bhagavan Krishna in the *Bhagavad Gita* gives a similar advice to Arjuna. He says, "I am giving you the greatest knowledge, which has never ever been given before, but treasure it well, don't give it to anybody." This means that it would be useless to give the *Guru Gita* to people who don't understand the importance of this knowledge. It would be a waste of time, a waste of effort. Like Christ said in *The Bible*, "Don't throw pearls to the pigs. They will trample over them not knowing their value."

Bhagavan Shankar is saying, "Don't give this secret! Don't reveal it to people who don't understand, who don't have this aim. Don't give it to people, who in spite of hearing it, this will not make any changes inside of them." Is better you "keep it as a secret". And reveal this secret only to those who are worthy of it.

Verse 179

**Svāmi mukhya gaṇeśādi
viṣṇvādīnāṁ ca pārvati
Manasāpi na vaktavyaṁ
satyaṁ satyaṁ vadāmyaham**

Do not even think of imparting it even to Swami Kartikeya, Ganesha, Vishnu or any of my chief attendants. What I told you is the truth, the pure truth.

Here Shiva is saying, "O Parvati, what I am giving to you, what I am telling you, the secret of it, the deepness of it, don't reveal it to your own sons, Ganesha and Kartikeya. Don't reveal it to the devas." Why? Because they are direct devotees of the Supreme Lord Himself. They will not understand the importance of the Guru, because they are Svayam Gurus themselves. They are born Gurus. They are the manifested Gurus. The sages will not understand because they have been manifested as Gurus themselves. So there is no one higher than them to guide them. Whereas Shiva, who is a bhakta, He understands the secret. That's why Shiva is always meditating on the Feet of Narayana.

Verse 180

**Atīva pakvacittāya
śraddhā bhakti utāya ca
Pravaktavyamidaṁ devi
mamātmā'si sadā priye**

O Beloved, you are my very Self. Reveal it only to one whose mind is ripe and full of reverence and devotion to Me.

Bhagavan Shankar is saying, "Don't reveal it to anybody but to the "one whose mind is ripe", to the one who is ready, to the one who has full love and devotion to the Guru. They are worthy of such Grace, because whatever you give them, they will put into practice. Whereas the others, whatever you tell them, they will hear it as beautiful for the ears, they will say, "Yes, yes, yes, Swami! Beautiful!" And then, nothing happens.

It's like what Christ said to His disciples, that while sowing some of the seeds fall on stones and will not germinate; some fall in barren land, they will grow but will dry out afterwards. But when they fall on fertile land, they will grow and bear lots of fruits. They shall multiply.

Here Bhagavan Shiva is saying the same thing, "Don't impart that knowledge to everybody, but only to the ones who have Guru-bhakti inside of them!"

Even now here many have listened, but only few have really understood. Many have listened and had fallen asleep. They have not understood. They are not ready. But the ones who are truly absorbing the essence of it, the Guru-bhakti will also bear its fruits.

Verse 181

Abhakte vañcake dhūrte
pākhaṇḍe nāstike nare
Manasāpi na vaktavyā
guru gītā kadācana

Do not ever think in your heart of hearts of imparting the Guru Gita to one who is an unbeliever, a cheat, a degraded wretch, a hypocrite or an atheist.

Bhagavan Shiva is saying, "Don't by any means impart this knowledge to a hypocrite, because it is useless. Don't impart it to somebody who doesn't believe in the Guru seva. Don't impart it to an unbeliever. Don't impart it to a cheater." That's what Christ said, "Those who have ears to hear, let them hear. Those who have eyes to see, let them see."

Verse 182

Saṁsāra sāgara
samuddharaṇaika mantraṁ
Brahmādi deva muni
pūjita siddha mantram
Dāridray duḥkha bhava
roga vināśa mantraṁ
Vande mahābhayaharaṁ
guru rāja mantram

My salutations to the mantra, incantation, which is the only one that is capable of rescuing me from the sea of Samsara, family and the world; the mantra worshipped by Brahma, the deities and great seers; the mantra which is a remedy for all worldly maladies, poverty and grief; and the mantra which is the sovereign of all mantras and the dispeller of all dire and mighty fears.

"My salutations to the mantra, incantation, which is the only one that is capable of rescuing me from the sea of Samsara." This mantra is the name of the Guru. The mantra which saves is the aadesh, the word, the order of the Master. The mantra that saves is the dedication to the Guru, which frees one from the ocean of delusion, which frees one from "family and the world".

"The mantra worshipped by Brahma, the deities and great seers, the mantra which is a remedy for all worldly maladies, poverty and grief; and the mantra which is the sovereign of all mantras and the dispeller of all dire and mighty fears." That mantra is the name of the Guru. That mantra is the Guru Mantra. The mantra is the focus on the Guru.

Iti śrīskandapurāṇe

Here ends the Guru Gita.

uttarakhaṇḍe

īśvarapārvatīsaṁvāde gurugita samāptā
Sri Gurudev Mahavatar Babaji
arpanamastu.
Sri Gurudev Sri Ramanujacharya
arpanamastu.
Sri Gurudev Battarangacharya
arpanamastu.

Thus ends the Guru Gita, which occurs in the dialogue between Shiva and Parvati in the latter portion of the Skanda Purana. This is offered to all the Gurus, Mahavatar Babaji, Sri Ramanujaacharya and Sri Battarangacharya.

Satguru Maharaj Ki... Jai!

Satgurudev Sri Swami Vishwananda
Mahaprabhu Ki... Jai!

This is the *'Song of the Guru'*, the *Guru Gita*, the 182 praises to the Guru. There are 400 verses in the *Skanda Purana*, but the other verses are not that important. Only these verses say everything.

Now it's up to you.

Jai Gurudev!

The Essence of
Everything is

Just Love

Swami Vishwananda

Made in United States
Orlando, FL
12 May 2025

61219874R00179